CROSSCURRENTS *Modern Critiques*
Harry T. Moore, *General Editor*

Glenn S. Burne

Remy de Gourmont

HIS IDEAS AND INFLUENCE

IN ENGLAND AND AMERICA

WITH A PREFACE BY

Harry T. Moore

Carbondale

SOUTHERN ILLINOIS UNIVERSITY PRESS

For Jo

PREFACE

GLENN S. BURNE'S BOOK on Remy de Gourmont is a timely study of an author who is lately beginning to attract more attention than he has done for a number of years. It is a fine and important revaluation of a writer about whom everyone interested in modern literature will want to know more; this book provides the opportunity for knowing more about him, and it does so in two ways.

Mr. Burne deals not only with Gourmont's own work but, as his subtitle promises, with "his ideas and influence in England and America"—Mr. Burne accurately shows how important those ideas and that influence really were to various major authors. T. S. Eliot, whose own debt to Gourmont is indicated by Mr. Burne, once spoke of Gourmont as "the critical consciousness of a generation." He was one of the founding editors of the Mercure de France, which became the greatest French literary journal at the turn of the century, and he was the persuasive critical expositor of the symboliste movement. Above all, Gourmont was a typical literary man of a country that is perhaps almost too literary: he was one of those authors who are both honored and ignored, but whose funerals are public events. A public statue of Gourmont was erected in his native Normandy, at Coutances, where he had attended the lycée before studying law at the University of Caen. By 1922, seven years after Gourmont's death, his works were more widely read than those of any other French writer—a condition that has not continued.

Gourmont for many years hardly left his apartment on the rue des Saints-Pères because of an unusual disease which Mr. Burne tells of in the pages that follow; he also gives an account of Gourmont's amatory life, which seems to have been rather complicated, at once French and international. I'll leave all this to Mr. Burne, who does very well with it.

Beyond what I've said, I can add only that this book is a most welcome addition to the Crosscurrents series, for it is time to have a new and up-to-date view of Remy de Gourmont, who was once called "a descendent of the encyclopedists and renovated by Nietzsche." Gourmont's poetry, admittedly, belongs to a lost past, and Mr. Burne does little with it here except to mention it as a forerunner of vers libre and Imagism, and to quote a passage of Gourmont's verse above one of Ezra Pound's which may or may not have been influenced by it. Similarly, Mr. Burne pays little heed to Gourmont's fiction except as it embodies his ideas. But this book is deeply concerned with Gourmont's criticism, especially his writings about style (which influenced one of the finest recent English books on the subject, John Middleton Murry's The Problem of Style, whose very title is a translation from Gourmont). And, as I have noted, Mr. Burne examines Gourmont's effect on recent English and American literature.

One of those influenced by this French author was Richard Aldington, whose long poem A Dream in the Luxembourg bears a close kinship to the title of one of Gourmont's novels (really a dialogue), Une Nuit au Luxembourg. Aldington knew Gourmont very well by correspondence but had just missed meeting him: a letter from Gourmont to the young Aldington on Bastille Day 1913 expresses regret that the English visitor hadn't appeared at the rue des Saints-Pères at four in the afternoon, because Gourmont had to go out at five, by which time Aldington hadn't turned up. After the war broke out, and Gourmont was in need, Aldington, acting as a free-lance agent without pay, helped him by selling his writings to British and American magazines. After Gourmont's death in September 1915 there was a dispute between his sister-in-law, Mme. Jean de Gourmont, and one of his mistresses, the Mme. de Courrières whom Mr. Burne will mention later, as to who should receive whatever funds might still come in: a rather typical French imbroglio. Aldington, acting in British fashion, courteously mailed each of the ladies a letter of condolence and sent the money in care of Gourmont's account with the Mercure de France.

Thirteen years later, when Aldington translated and edited a two-volume anthology of de Gourmont, he felt that he had made use of everything worth preserving from Gourmont's voluminous work. "The best of it is so good," Aldington said later, "that no one who cares for European literature should miss it." As Mr. Burne's bibliography in the present book indicates, Chatto and Windus in 1932 brought out a one-volume redaction of the Aldington translation. I hope that Mr. Burne's book will once again call attention to Gourmont's writings; and some paperback publisher might do well by making the Aldington anthology available again.

HARRY T. MOORE

May 24, 1963

ACKNOWLEDGMENTS

I WISH TO THANK the following persons who read the manuscript and made valuable suggestions: Dr. Jackson Mathews of the Bollingen Foundation, Dr. Martin Nurmi of Kent State University, and Dr. Alex Fischler of the University of Oregon. I also wish to acknowledge two esteemed precursors, Professors Garnett Rees and J. D. R. Mossop, whose earlier studies of Gourmont have been most helpful to me in my own work, and to thank Professor John J. Espey of the University of California (Los Angeles) for his useful suggestions. To the Research Committee of Kent State University I am grateful for a grant-in-aid for travel and typing.

Parts of Chapter 2 appeared in *The Western Humanities Review*, XIII (Winter 1959), as "Remy de Gourmont: A Scientific Philosophy of Art," and part of Chapter 4 in the *Bucknell Review*, VIII (February 1959), as "T. S. Eliot and Remy de Gourmont." Both are reprinted here with permission.

CONTENTS

Remy de Gourmont
HIS IDEAS AND INFLUENCE
IN ENGLAND AND AMERICA

1   THE MAN

"MY GENERATION needed Remy de Gourmont," Ezra Pound wrote in 1934, and Richard Aldington, looking back on the literary situation before World War I, posed the question: "Why was the name of 'Remy de Gourmont' so potent, so sure of our respect?"

In the 1960's a reader of English and American literature written during the first twenty-five years of this century is apt to ask a somewhat different question: "Who was Remy de Gourmont, anyway?" It is one of the recognized vagaries of literary history that the leading lights of one era, when caught in the shifting currents of literary fashion, often dim to the point of near-extinction in the next. Remy de Gourmont, one of the most brilliant and erudite minds of the period from 1885 to 1915, exerted a profound influence on English and American writers of the subsequent generation and evoked immoderate praise and an even greater tribute—emulation and discipleship—from authors, some of whom have grown to major stature in our own times. Gourmont, as an editor of the influential *Mercure de France* and author of more than forty volumes of works in all genres, commanded considerable respect in his native France, and, as is sometimes the case in international literary relations, achieved an even greater fame and respect abroad. In France he was but one of many; in England and America he was chosen as the ideal man of letters by a considerable group of aspiring authors: he was a scholarly artist of proven courage and devotion

to the highest standards of art and so possessed the very
qualities sought by young writers earnestly looking for a
prestigious guide and prophet in their own struggles to establish a "new" literature. T. S. Eliot was much "stimulated and helped" by Gourmont's critical writings; the
iconoclastic works of Pound and Aldington abound in
studies and translations of their French precursor; Middleton Murry's *The Problem of Style* owes much more to
Gourmont's *Le Problème du Style* than the title; René
Taupin's book, *L'Influence du Symbolisme français sur la
Poésie américaine, 1910–1920,* mentions the name of
Remy de Gourmont more often than the name of any
other French writer. Speaking of the early years of the
vers-libre movement, Sir Herbert Read has recently remarked: "The guiding critic was Remy de Gourmont,
whose *Livre des Masques* had given definition to the
whole movement, and whose *Problème du Style* is a
source-book for many of the ideas that inspired the literary
developments in both France and England at this time.
I am afraid it has been forgotten how much we all owed
to this brilliant critic. Pound was in direct communication
with him until his death." [1]

Today, surprisingly little is known of Gourmont in this
country, or in France, for that matter, where he seems to
be considered by most students of modern literature as
something *démodé,* perhaps as representative of a literary
world that died, along with much else associated with
"The Banquet Years," during the grim period of 1914–18.
In recent years, however, we have seen in this country and
in England a growing awareness of the rich contribution
of French Symbolism to the formation of our own literature, an awareness stimulated by superior translations as
well as by revealing scholarly studies of modern French
writers. Poets and critics like Baudelaire, Laforgue,
Corbière, Apollinaire, and Valéry are now being heralded
as precursors worthy of our consideration, as writers whose
works must be known if full understanding of our own
writers is to be gained. And today, after having been
largely ignored for the last twenty-five years, Remy de

Gourmont's essays are being either included or discussed in recent anthologies of critical writing, such as those edited by Ray B. West and Eric Bentley. However, these are necessarily fragmentary pieces; they can reveal only a limited view of a writer whose works cover, with varying degrees of authority, a great variety of subjects. In fact, Kenneth Burke has remarked that, when Gourmont started writing seriously (in the 1890's), so vigorous was his activity that there soon circulated the rumor in Parisian literary circles that Remy de Gourmont was a group of writers using one pseudonym.

Although he wrote poetry, plays, stories and novels, Gourmont was essentially an essayist, a critic. He possessed undeniable artistic talent, but this faculty was subordinated to the rational mind. His artistry was employed in the service of his theories of art and human conduct; his imaginative works can be seen as dramatizations of the ideas expressed in his philosophical and critical essays.

As critic, Gourmont's interests and knowledge ranged from Provençal and medieval Latin poetry to contemporary literature and included the authors of foreign nations; he was an able if at times imperfect translator from the Spanish, Italian, Latin and English. Also, he produced notable studies in psychology, philology, and philosophy. He was a talented amateur in physiology and zoology, and a perceptive commentator on day-to-day affairs. These varied writings, which Ezra Pound characterized as "the best portrait available, the best record that is, of the civilized mind from 1885 to 1915," fill over forty volumes and present a formidable problem to a scholar desiring to find, or to impose, a semblance of order. Seekers after systems will find Gourmont an exasperating subject. He contradicted himself often, sometimes openly, rarely with regret; he did not hesitate to change sides in an argument if he felt the weight of evidence to have shifted, and he treated issues of great gravity with an air of either indulgent or mocking irony. The last thing Gourmont wanted to do was to found a "school" or create a system.

Thus Gourmont's readers are confronted by a multifaceted personality and a mind of great complexity which, nonetheless, sought a unity of intelligence through the interpenetration of disciplines and the breakdown of boundaries. Like Taine, Renan, and Anatole France, Gourmont combined in one person the qualities of an artist, a scientist, a critic, and a philosopher. He made a valiant and stimulating attempt, after the manner of the eighteenth-century Encyclopedists, to synthesize all the important currents of thought of the period into an up-to-date and hence reliable foundation for evaluating the products of the human mind; to bring the findings of science, psychology and philosophy to bear on the problems of art and human conduct. Perhaps this attempt falls into the category of "magnificent failures"; perhaps Aldington is correct in observing that the very grandiose-ness of Gourmont's venture, by dissipating his undeniable talents over too great an area, only insured his lack of success; but it did not prevent his producing one of the richest storehouses of erudition and critical commentary in modern literature, of which our English and American writers have used but a small part.

It was Gourmont's very diversity and richness of mind that enabled writers and scholars of varying tastes to find in him a source of intellectual nourishment and inspiration. It enabled T. E. Hulme and T. S. Eliot to be influenced by his aristocratic concept of art, his studies of sensibility and style, while they ignored his skepticism, materialism, and avowed hostility to orthodoxy and dogma of any kind. Similarly F. S. Flint could be interested in Gourmont's writings on free verse; Ezra Pound could praise his early Symbolist poems for their suggestiveness, sonority and rhythms, and join the other Imagists in citing his later emphasis on hardness, concision, and directness in poetry. Aldous Huxley, one of Gourmont's translators, imitated the sensual intellectualism of Gourmont's novels, whereas both Pound and Aldington found in him an apostle of freedom and literary iconoclasm. Although later impressionist critics cited Gourmont as an illustrious predecessor, scholars admired his erudition and "sense of fact"; Kenneth Burke studied his writings on language and the "dissociation of ideas"; Havelock Ellis praised his writings on psychology and the physical sciences, while acknowledging him the leading aesthetician of the Symbolist movement; and all his readers, regardless of their special interests, respected his integrity, his intelligence, and his devotion to the profession of scholarship and letters.

But a reader might ask, is Gourmont all complexity, all diversity? A careful study of his works reveals a consistent substratum of thought underlying his apparently contradictory assertions. There is a solid Gourmont, intact and coherent, behind his many facets. There is no "system," but rather a persistent point of view: if one were to take the numerous quotations, references, and epigraphs derived from Gourmont's writings, which adorn the pages of English and American writers, and trace them back to their source, they would be found to be more than mere shining bits of quotable wisdom, useful as critical gambits leading into one's own essays. They would prove to be elements from a large and complicated structure of thought, lacking clear outlines and formal organization, but based on certain fundamental concepts slowly pieced together by Gourmont between the years 1885 and 1915. These concepts "evolved"—that is, they changed superficially, were expanded or modified, but they remain essentially the same and as such form the foundations on which Gourmont's entire creative and critical writings are based. Moreover, his novels, plays, and poetry, though possessing inherent weaknesses as autonomous works of art, take on considerable importance in relation to the whole of Gourmont's production. They are, on one hand, "exercises" in clarifying his own ideas, and on the other hand, maneuvers in a war of literary theories, and as such are worthy of consideration. Inconsistencies and contradictions we will find, to be sure, as is almost inevitable in a writer as prolific as Gourmont; but they are more apparent than real and are referable to a consistent realm of values and basic principles which insure the integrity of Gourmont's many roles.

ii

Gourmont's life divides itself roughly into four periods. The first involves his rather obscure beginnings: he was learning to write, publishing "vulgarizations" and trying to find himself in the world of literature. The second is his Symbolist period, characterized on the one hand by an obsession for the exotic, the unusual, and the perverse, and on the other hand by the serious study of philosophy in the attempt to found a metaphysical basis for Symbolism. In this period he published most of his poetry, plays, and early novels, some scholarship, but little criticism. He was dominated by what Aldington has called the "Flaubertian maxim": "simply that the man of intelligence revenges himself upon a dull world by 'corrupting' it." Gourmont spread hatred into his works—hatred of the commonplace, the bourgeois, the mediocre—"but he came to realize that there is more in literature than mere disgust, however brilliant."

In his third period Gourmont began his critical work, writing his retrospective interpretations of the Symbolist movement and developing his latent interest in science. He ceased to desire the "perversion of the world," but retained from the earlier period his sense of irony, his love of good writing, and his hatred of sham. He became obsessed with "truth" and sought always to express himself clearly and honestly, even at the expense of frequent apparent self-contradiction. This period carries over into the fourth, after the turn of the century, when he produced his fine studies in aesthetics and style, his best criticism in the *Promenades*, and his lively writings on science. Gourmont's true biography is his collected works, and his collected works make an invaluable intellectual history of his period.

Gourmont was born in Normandy, in the Château de La Motte, at Bazoches-en-Houlme (Orne) on April 4,

1858. He was descended from an old family, noted principally as printers and engravers, dating back to the sixteenth century. During the seventeenth and eighteenth centuries the Gourmonts were Norman country gentry of the minor nobility, having connections with the Catholic Church. Young Remy attended the Lycée at Coutances and the Law School of the University of Caen. His instructors characterized him at that time as having a distinguished but undisciplined mind, and as tending to make excursions into fantasy. This was a very perceptive prognosis of a characteristic which was to govern Gourmont's work, for better and worse, throughout his life.

Coming to Paris in 1883 at the age of twenty-five, Gourmont took a position as assistant librarian at the Bibliothèque Nationale and settled down to a life of study and the writing of "vulgarizations" on diverse subjects. Three things of importance happened to him during this period. First, he made several personal contacts which were to influence greatly his literary attitudes. Through Villiers de l'Isle-Adam he came to know J.-K. Huysmans, whose *À Rebours* (1884) was to be reflected in Gourmont's work for the next decade. At this same time Gourmont became infatuated with Madame Berthe de Courrière, a strange and colorful figure reputed to have been a dabbler in the occult arts and an adept of the Black Mass; she is supposed to have introduced Gourmont's friend Huysmans into the Satanic activities taking place in and around Paris.[2] She was probably the original for Huysmans' Mme. Chantelouve in *Là-Bas* and there is little doubt that she was the "Sixtine" after whom Gourmont titled one novel and volume of published letters. She provided inspiration and characterization, but it was to Huysmans that the young Gourmont owed his early tastes in literature and precious prose style. Along with Villiers de l'Isle-Adam, Huysmans was the most important literary influence of Gourmont's early years. It took the younger man nearly a decade to work free of a model whose influence, it must be concluded, was often a serious hindrance to his intellectual development.

The second important incident of this period is what Gourmont's commentators have called his "facial drama." While still in his mid-twenties Gourmont contracted a disease, a revolting skin ailment similar to leprosy and called "lupus," which so disfigured and discolored his face as to make him nearly unrecognizable. It gave him the appearance, according to Paul Léautaud, "of a gnome and an old man." Léautaud, who knew Gourmont personally during this period, said that for several years Gourmont dared go out only in the evening and then only for a short distance; he visited no one, and received no one except his brother Jean. The extent of his disfigurement was painfully dramatized on one occasion. After having been in Paris about ten years without seeing his family, Gourmont was obliged to return home to visit his sick mother. When he arrived with his brother at the railroad station near the family home, they were met by their father, who failed utterly to recognize his eldest son. The old man turned immediately to Jean and asked, "But where is Remy? Did he not come?" [3]

Léautaud assures us—rather unconvincingly—that Gourmont's disease did not make him really ugly—though he took a bit of getting used to.[4] But he believed that the malady greatly affected Gourmont's attitudes; it was the cause of his intense "disdain" and his "frenetic sensuality, that of an ardent man condemned to chastity." Jean de Gourmont took exception to this view, maintaining that there was nothing exceptional about his brother's "mépris" and that the tragedy had not shaken Remy's native optimism. To this Léautaud replied that it was the optimism of a man "who finds that all is well because nothing deserves to be better." Doctor Paul Voivenel, who treated Gourmont during the first stages of his illness and remained his life-long friend, tended to side with brother Jean in this matter. He stated that after the first few years Gourmont resumed a normal, if somewhat limited, sex life, and that he was by no means condemned to a miserable life of enforced chastity; that as Gourmont's fame grew his position as a writer of note gave him a

charm which, in the ladies' eyes, far outweighed his facial
shortcomings, and that, furthermore, history offers many
an example of a Don Juan whose success in love was
matched only by his personal ugliness—that, in short,
many women are sexually attracted by the ill favored.[5]

Be that as it may, there can be little doubt that Gourmont's tragedy aggravated, if it did not create, certain
traits latent in him. He had already shown reclusive
tendencies, for he was a *contemplatif*, a man of ideas not
of action, aloof and disdainful, and his disfigurement
seemed to intensify those tendencies to the point where
he retired into almost total solitude. But the most important result can be seen in terms of a certain intellectual
sensuality; he became what Garnet Rees calls "un cérébral
sensuel." Gourmont had always believed in solitude as the
best manner of preserving his individualism, but solitude is
obviously at odds with the fulfillment of sensual desires.
One critic said of Gourmont that "the intensity of his
cerebral life is but a function of the intensity of his
sexual life" and adds that these two sides of human nature
were reciprocally intensified in Gourmont, who "confessed" both sides without compunction or dissimulation.[6]
His early writings, especially his novels and stories, display
a frank obsession with sexuality which, however, reveals
no trace of wistfulness or "sour grapes." Gourmont's
philosophy of pleasure was the "mysticisme du Désir et de
la Volupté," and in view of his actual life was the highest
form of heroism; for despite the cruelty of the "facial
drama," he continued to affirm the pleasure of living.

The third important event of this period completed
the circle of solitude drawing about him: he was dismissed
from his job at the Bibliothèque Nationale for having
written a rather sharp attack on the extreme patriotism current in France at the time. In an article, "Le Jou-jou
patriotisme," *Mercure de France*, April, 1891, Gourmont
protested against the prevailing anti-German sentiment—
"revanche"—and the extreme concern over Alsace-Lor-
raine, and came out in favor of international amity and
understanding. Hostility from the Paris press, especially

from one Henri Fouquier of *l'Echo de Paris,* cost Gourmont his job.[7] As this happened about the same time as his facial disaster, Gourmont retired from society and lived out the rest of his life as a sort of literary anchorite, isolated except for the attentions of his mistress, Mme. de Courrière, who lived in a neighboring flat. She continued a close relationship with him, even after the appearance, in later years, of the second woman in Gourmont's life, Natalie Clifford Barney, "Amazone."

During the late 1880's Gourmont remained aloof from current literary movements, preferring to devote himself to a study of the classics. It is interesting to note that the future spokesman for one of the most avant-garde of literary schools found modern poetry, with its "painful verbal researches," to be "an aberration of taste" and not worthy of his attention.

Then he suddenly discovered Symbolism. He tells how one afternoon, quite by chance, browsing through a copy of Mallarmé's *La Vogue,* he was immediately captivated by what he described as a new "aesthetic tremor" and an exquisite impression of novelty which left him filled with disgust for what he had previously written. In less than an hour, he tells us, his literary orientation was radically modified.[8] This experience, along with his friendship with Huysmans and Villiers de l'Isle-Adam, completed his conversion to Symbolism.

In January of 1890 Gourmont was one of the founders of the *Mercure de France,* a literary journal destined to become during the next few years the rallying point of the new Symbolist movement. Under the directorship of Alfred Vallette the *Mercure* did not at first present any positive credo, but conducted an assault on the *status quo* in literature and ideas. By 1893, however, it had become the official Symbolist organ, largely as a result of the influence of Charles Morice and Gourmont.[9] For, while he was only one of the editors of the journal, Gourmont had considerable prestige and much to say about the magazine's policy. According to Henri de Regnier, Gourmont had great authority and influence at the *Mercure* offices;

his colleagues showed tremendous respect for his erudition, penetration, and sound judgment. "Remy de Gourmont is a great writer," says Regnier. "He is our Montaigne, our Sainte-Beuve. He is our Gourmont." [10]

So for the rest of his life Gourmont divided his time between his book-stocked rooms in the rue des Saints-Pères and the nearby offices of the *Mercure de France,* a studious life varied by occasional evening strolls and book-hunting excursions among the "bouquinistes" along the banks of the Seine. During the first half of the 1890's he wrote little criticism, devoting his time to scholarship and the writing of novels, short stories, plays and poetry, all in the Symbolist manner. Most of these early works appeared in elegantly designed, deluxe limited editions. At that time he was not much interested in being widely read, sharing as he did the Symbolist disdain for the masses, but he did love beautiful books. He thought them especially attractive when they contained words of a bizarre and novel flavor. During this early period his interest had turned to the Middle Ages, and he developed a scholarly as well as artistic interest in words. His friendship for Huysmans and his reading À *Rebours* were reflected in a growing taste for the out-of-the-way in style and attitude. Indeed, his choice of reading seemed derived from Huysmans' Des Esseintes—the writers of the Latin Decadence, the mystic poets of the Latin Middle Ages, the lesser-known poets of the Renaissance. He developed a contempt for the Neo-classic period and the eighteenth century, and a great admiration for Baudelaire, Mallarmé, and Lautréamont. He preferred writers of a bold and original bent and poetry of perverse and naïve images. In 1894, in collaboration with Alfred Jarry, he began publishing an elegant review, *l'Ymagier,* offering a mélange of the most primitive "images d'Epinal" along with designs by Whistler, Gauguin, de Groux, d'Espagnat, Séguin, Filiger, some Durer engravings, a lithograph by Rousseau, and woodcuts and commentaries by Jarry and himself. He did not write much original material for this publication but revived old masterpieces like "Le Mystère

Théophile," "Aucassin et Nicolette," and "Patience de Grisélidis." A curious publication, l'Ymagier did not last long, but it became the model to be followed by other magazines, wherein Gourmont published more works in the vein of l'Ymagier—such short pieces as Phocas, Poésie populaire, and Le Miracle de Théophile de Rutebeuf.

The principal work to come out of Gourmont's medi-evalist period was Le Latin mystique (1892), an anthology of late medieval mystic Latin poets, with translations and commentaries. The preface was written by Huysmans, who used the space allotted to him mainly to attack the "pseudo-mysticism" of the nineteenth century (mysticism, he said, rightfully belongs to the Church) and to display his growing lack of sympathy for the Symbolist movement. He found fault with Gourmont's translations and ignored the literary aim of the work, which was—and this is a basic tenet of Gourmont criticism—to find new reasons for read-ing old literature. Gourmont was looking for, and claimed to find, certain analogies between medieval Latin litera-ture and literary tendencies of his own time. This work was a notable contribution to Symbolism, emphasizing as it did the rhythms and musical quality of the Latin verse, and its symbolic use of flowers and jewels. It also had a direct influence on Gourmont's own poetry: the Litanies de la Rose and Les Saints du Paradis were inspired by and written in emulation of the medieval poets, especially Goddeschalk.

The personal element in Gourmont's Litanies is, how-ever, easily identified, for although he adopted the forms and long harmonious phrases of liturgy, his subject is one of delicate blasphemy. A tone of invocation expresses a disdain of the religious spirit, an equivocal mixture of artifice and spontaneity, of chastity and voluptuousness, of the boudoir and the confessional. Gourmont himself commented on this tendency in a study of Maeterlinck: "One of the most curious characteristics of the symbolist movement is the acceptance of religious forms of thought combined with a complete disdain for all religious spirit." [11]

Aside from this blasphemous element, Gourmont has little to say in his poetry. At that time he was interested only in the sounds of words, not their meanings—a temporary, extreme Symbolist view. His poems in verse, *Hiéroglyphes* (1894), are reminiscent of those of his favorite modern poets, Baudelaire and Mallarmé, but the writing of poetry was for him a mere game, a "jeu de mots," experiments with the possibilities of sound and rhythm, not intended to be in the least "sincere." His poems were not taken very seriously by either himself or his readers. (Though they did have some effect on his Anglo-American followers, especially Ezra Pound, who found much to praise in the *Litanies de la Rose* and *Fleurs de Jadis*.) In fact, in the preface to his collected poems, significantly called *Divertissements*, he refuted the need for sincerity in poetry. His stories and plays are serious efforts, but not his poetry, which lacks true feeling, true poetic impulse, and reflects Gourmont's usual serenity and detachment, evincing not so much a lack of sensibility as a predominance of intellect over sensibility. His intelligence, always seeking the most savory "divertissement," seems to direct and fashion the sensibility to its own tastes, for Gourmont was an artist for whom the play of intelligence was the supreme satisfaction. Perhaps a prime function of his writing poetry was to afford himself a pleasant respite from the scholarly study of philosophy that demanded most of his attention during the last half of the 1890's. His later verse does, however, contain much less pure verbalism, reflecting what was in fact a real change in attitude towards words, for from about 1897 on Gourmont became increasingly interested in science, philosophy, and the meanings of words. He no longer "collected" words but rather studied them from a scientific and historical point of view—an interest that enabled him to make such notable contributions to philology and rhetoric as *L'Esthétique de la Langue française*, the influential *Problème du Style*, and his well-known essay on the "Dissociation des Idées."

Gourmont's stories, written mostly during the early

1890's, emphasize the theme of sexuality versus the ideal. In their preoccupation with the perverse, and in their style—a curious mixture of preciosity and irony—they clearly show the influence of Huysmans and Villiers: elegance combined with a ferocious irony, and a heavy emphasis on sexuality, which is Gourmont's own bent. Because of this latter element, some critics see Gourmont as a descendent of Laclos and de Sade, but surely he needed no guides in this realm. He wrote most of his stories during the period 1891–95, when he was suffering from the first shock of facial disfigurement, cut off, for a time at least, from normal sexual relations, his only female companion being Mme. de Courrière, who was then in the thick of her Black Mass activities and could hardly be looked to as a stabilizing influence.[12] As his stories are full of various forms of sadistic eroticism and religious sacrilege, Gourmont has also been lumped with the Satanists,[13] who were so very prevalent in those days, but there is something to Kenneth Burke's observation that Gourmont's blasphemy was not mere insolence or cheap derision; rather it was the expression of religious inclination in an intelligence that could not believe: "Since it is impossible to praise the divinities with sincerity, there is nothing left but to insult them." [14] Be that as it may, Gourmont's short stories earned him the reputation of a frivolous "erotomane." This label, given him during his early years, tended to obscure his later and more important works, and many readers still know him by it today.

Gourmont's novels, like his stories and plays, were experiments in working out ideas and theories, dramatizations of the opinions expressed in his essays. For Gourmont was fundamentally an essayist, a philosopher, and a critic. He loved to manipulate ideas—he played with them, fondled them almost sensually, cast them into different forms to see how they would perform. That he was also an artist is shown by the excellence of his style, the subtlety of his perceptions, and the refinement of his sensibility; but his artistry was destined ultimately to serve his ideas, a means of exploring and clarifying his thoughts and giving them concrete form. His novels are extremely subjective, at times "confessional," and the characters are easily identified as aspects of the author's own sensibility. Generally, his fiction has two main, closely related themes: sexuality and the philosophy of subjective idealism. That is, the world is representation and perception is often hallucination, and woman is the "creation" of the man who loves her. She is a force which restrains man when he seeks the infinite, and her identity is but the result of that man's love. The theme of mysticism versus carnality, in one form or another, runs through all of Gourmont's plays and fiction. Woman appears as "the artful creature that humiliates man by securing him with carnal chains." [15] This view of woman does not seem to conflict, in Gourmont's mind, with his view of sexuality: "Chastity is a sexual aberration, a crime against nature." This theme, which he developed "scientifically" in the *Physique de l'Amour, Essai sur l'instinct sexuel* (1903), runs through all his later novels—*Les Chevaux de Diomède* (1897), *Le Songe d'une Femme* (1899), *Une Nuit au Luxembourg* (1906), and *Un Coeur virginal* (1907)— and will be discussed more fully in the next chapter when we come to consider Gourmont's philosophy.

In November 1895, Gourmont began a series of short articles in the *Mercure de France* which became the *Epilogues* published in book form later. Each issue contained ironic or mocking comments on the deeds and ideas of the day and gave an interesting picture of intellectual developments from 1895 to 1915. These articles marked an important shift in Gourmont's interests, as they dealt with ordinary, everyday subjects and were written in a simple, direct style. From this point on the *style alambiqué* and esoteric subject-matter belonged to the past. He progressively shook off the influence of the "Decadents" and was attracted increasingly to science and philology. He even co-operated with Edouard Dujardin and the biologist René Quinton in founding the *Revue des Idées*, a journal dedicated to a *rapprochement* of science and the arts. He retained his love of the "beau style" from the time of Symbolism, but he came to study it more from a rhetorical and psychological point of view.

Gourmont produced his best works of literary criticism and science after 1899. In 1896 and 1898 he had published his two *Livres des Masques*, essays of critical introductions to the Symbolist poets, but neither of these books attained the level of the later works: the *Esthètique de la Langue française* (1899), *La Culture des Idées* (1900), *Le Problème du Style* (1902), the *Physique de l'Amour* (1903), and the two series of collected essays, the *Promenades littéraires* and *Promenades philosophiques*, which appeared periodically from 1904 until after Gourmont's death in 1915.

Some of the best writing of Gourmont's last years is found in the two volumes, *Lettres à l'Amazone* (1914) and *Lettres intimes à l'Amazone*, which appeared posthumously in 1926. Both were inspired by the enchanting young poetess, Miss Natalie Clifford Barney, who had come from America to conduct a literary salon, attended principally by female poets, somewhat after the manner of the famed Sappho. Besides luring the literary recluse out of hiding, even to the extent of attending one of her fancy-dress parties, she inspired Gourmont to write some of his most searching and provocative essays. The first book, *Lettres à l'Amazone*, though written in response to actual conversations with Miss Barney, was intended from the start for publication; but the volume of *Letters intimes* was not, and it reveals an unsuspected Gourmont. In place of the usual surveying of man's follies with mocking irony, one finds revelations of personal suffering by a Gourmont of "tendresse"—revelations which lead one to wonder to what extent the public pose was just a mask.

The closing years of Gourmont's life were full of bitterness and frustration. Ill health, the shock of World War I, lack of money resulting from the closing down of magazine publication—all combined to make his life difficult and to hasten its end. His writing during the war years reflected a loss of poise, of that detachment and serenity which had given his work its unique value. But during the second year of the war Gourmont regained much of his composure and gathered together his scholarly faculties for another major study, *Physique des Moeurs,* which was to have been a sequel to *Physique de l'Amour.* Death, however, intervened. Gourmont suffered a stroke on September 25, 1915, and died two days later.

When the news of his death reached America, eulogies poured into the little magazines. "Gourmont is dead," Ezra Pound wrote, "and the world's light is darkened." In 1919 *The Little Review* issued a special Gourmont number, in which Aldington wrote, "He seemed much more of our generation than many contemporaries. He seemed the young man and they the past. . . . We have lost almost the last of the true critics."

> Le symbolisme fut avant tout une esthètique. Seul peut-
> être, l'auteur des Livres des Masques s'inquièta de lui
> donner une signification philosophique.
>
> —André Gide

IN MARCH 1893 Gourmont gathered together under the
title of *Idéalisme* several short articles which had been
published in various magazines during the preceding
spring. In a brief preface, spiced with the arrogance and
dogmatism typical of his early period of embattled Symbolism, he stated that the idealist theories were no longer
contested except by certain mediocrities in the Naturalist
camp. Nevertheless, he gives a defense of philosophical
idealism, beginning, as usual, with an assault on current
bourgeois concepts of the word "idealism," finding them
sentimental, "spiritualistic," or romantic. On the contrary, said Gourmont (and here we have an example of
his self-imposed mission as "sower of doubts," as destroyer
of false idols), true idealism is "an immoral and desperate
doctrine; anti-social and anti-human. And for that very
reason idealism is a very commendable doctrine, at a time
when it is not a question of preserving, but of destroying."

Since the fallible senses stand between man's consciousness and external phenomena, one can never truly know
those phenomena in themselves—only their "representa-
tions." Thus, "the only reality is thought." Knowing that
the individual is a world unto himself and that the external
world exists as a projection of his own consciousness, the

idealist can admit but one kind of government—anarchy —and he must ignore all "practical relativities" such as morality, sociability, the father-land, traditions, family, procreation, and so on.

With social life being thus ruled out of bounds, there remains but one domain where the idealist can function, indeed where he can flourish, and that is the domain of Art. However, Gourmont felt obliged to warn the reader that, art being so suspect in these philistine days, it must be practiced in secret, "in catacombs, like the first Christians, like the last pagans."

It was at this time that Gourmont made one of his first statements on Symbolism, an essay that appeared in the *Idéalisme* volume, in which he attempted to put the new movement on a philosophical basis and to justify some of its extremist aspects. After first distinguishing between two classes, those who have talent, "the Symbolists," and those who do not, "the Others," Gourmont dismissed the latter as out-of-date, principally because a major element in art is "the New." The fact that Symbolism gives free rein to an artist's originality was one of its chief charms to Gourmont. And Symbolism gives free rein because it "is translated literally by the word Liberty and, for the violent, by the word Anarchy." Art must break the chains, all rules and all formulas.

In order to show in what way Symbolism is "a theory of liberty," that is, how the term, contrary to anything strict and precise, implies an absolute license of ideas and forms, Gourmont emphasized the close rapport between Symbolism and Idealism:

> Idealism signifies the free and personal development of the intellectual individual in the intellectual series. Symbolism can (and even must) be considered by us as the free and personal development of the esthetic individual in the esthetic series, and the symbols which he will imagine or explicate will be imagined or explicated according to the special conception of the world morphologically possible to each symbolizing brain.[1]

A striking thing about this passage, as Martin Turnell points out, is that the critic has formulated his standards in terms of technical philosophy. Whereas an English critic like Matthew Arnold would propose as a test of poetry its "high seriousness" or would see its value as "a criticism of life," Gourmont used terms like "free and personal development of the intellectual individual in the intellectual series" and "world morphologically possible to each symbolizing brain." This difference in terms, Turnell tells us, came about because technical philosophy was still a part of the normal curriculum in French secondary schools, whereas scarcely any Englishman studied the subject.[2] Be that as it may, one must agree with Turnell in his statement that the influence of philosophy on nineteenth-century French criticism was "decisive."

Scholars are by no means agreed, however, that nineteenth-century French critics had assimilated or properly understood the various philosophies on which they based their aesthetic theories. The Symbolist writers were often guilty of misconstruing their philosophical sources and even of distorting them, if need be, to suit their own immediate poetical or critical purposes. A. G. Lehmann, for example, in his penetrating study, *The Symbolist Aesthetic in France, 1885–1895,* argues that the German idealist philosophers, who contributed so much to French Symbolist theories, were in fact ill-understood and poorly represented in France. The European literary world after 1870, Lehman points out, was divided roughly into two camps: the positivist, realist, naturalist; and the speculative, idealist, anti-naturalist. The first camp was largely French: Comte, Littré, Renan, Taine, the physio-psychologists, evolutionary biologists, and some historians. The other camp was mainly German: Fichte, Schelling, Kant, Hegel, Schopenhauer, all of whom, but especially the last three, enjoyed a great vogue in France during the last three-quarters of the nineteenth century. During this period there were many translations of major German figures, but not of the lesser figures nor of the great body of critical controversy which grew up around the major philosophers. To the French writer of the 1880's, "Kant and Schopenhauer were simply idealists: enormous figures, whose work, seen through a mist, appeared only in the vaguest outline." [3]

Most French writers lacked solid knowledge of German idealism; hence, it was "inevitable that the writings of the German philosophers, like massive lumps of authority to be thrown about, should be simple playthings invoked in arguments in no way resembling those which they had been developed out of and designed to deal with." The wave of national disillusionment and frustration which engulfed France after the Franco-Prussian War gave rise to an atmosphere highly receptive to German philosophical pessimism; Schopenhauer became exceedingly popular during the 1880's and 1890's, and his name was often invoked in support of the developing literary idealism. Lehmann, seeing Gourmont as an excellent example of distorted Schopenhauerism, cites the following excerpt from the Preface to the *Livres des Masques* (1896):

A new truth . . . which has recently made its appearance in literature and art, is entirely metaphysical, à priori (in appearance), and quite young, since it is only a century old and truly new, and since it has not yet done service in any esthetic order. This truth—evangelical and marvelous, liberating and renovating—is the principle of the ideal nature of the world. In relation to man, the thinking subject, the world—all that is external to the self—exists only as the idea formed of it. We know only phenomena; we can reason only about appearances. All truth, in itself, escapes us; the essence is unattainable. It is what Schopenhauer has popularized in that clear and simple formula: the world is my representation. I do not see what is; what is, is what I see. So many thinking men—so many diverse and perhaps different worlds.

Lehmann calls this "selective misinterpretation" and sees other cases of "solipsis and myth" in Edouard Dujardin, Téodor de Wyzewa, André Gide, right down to Valéry's *Monsieur Teste*, including Villiers de l'Isle-Adam —considered by many of his followers to be an authority on German idealism. In all those writers contributing to the Symbolist aesthetic, there was little real resemblance to Hegel and Schopenhauer. In French hands German idealism became, not a view of nature or phenomena, but "a system of valuation of experiences." Villiers' idealism was not related to a theory of knowledge but to a "psychology of conviction," and it contained more of poetry and myth than of clarity and precision. Symbolist idealism was rather the visions of prophets than the theories of philosophers.[4]

This is, of course, as it should be. The Symbolists were, after all, artists and critics, not philosophers. They sought sources of inspiration and creation as well as bases of aesthetic doctrine. Lehmann perceives this, and, despite his rather reprimanding tone, grants that Villiers' *Axël* and *Claire Lenoir*, like Gourmont's *Sixtine* and *Chevaux de Diomède*, are to be justified as artistic creations in conscious opposition to the tenets of naturalism, for these artists were attempting to introduce a new way of writing and so had recourse to prevailing philosophies as a way of combating theories of art generally accepted by the public. To most French writers of the time, idealism meant simply the inalienable right to interpret the world in whatever way one pleased, or to invent worlds possessing as much validity as the "common-sense" world and deserving the same respect from the point of view of art or of anything else.

One of Gourmont's main objectives that was dependent on his establishing the idealistic basis of Symbolism was his desire to provide a philosophical defense of obscurity and difficulty in much of the new poetry. Although Symbolism appeared in some ways to be a return to simplicity and clarity, it required, for its effects, a certain complexity and obscurity.[5] This is because "personal art," the *only* art according to Gourmont, is nearly always incomprehensible: "Understood, it ceases to be pure art and becomes a motif, a theme, for new expressions of art." But however personal symbolist art might be, it must in some way express the nonpersonal, if only to justify its name, and it must always be logical. Furthermore, it must "inquire into the permanent significance of transitory facts, and try to posit it—without conflicting with the exigencies of one's real vision"; that is, it must seek the Eternal in the shifting diversity of forms, the Truth concealed in passing False, the perennial Logic in the "illogic of the instant."

Gourmont foresaw possible objections here, for he hastened to admit that by the very definition of Idealism the Permanent cannot be conceived except as personal, as transitory, and that any true Absolute, if it exists, is unknowable and cannot be formulated in symbols. So he concludes his essay with a compromise in favor of the "relative Absolute": "It is therefore toward the relative absolute that Symbolism aims, to establish what it can of the eternal in the personal."

The preface to *Le Livre des Masques* (1896), which was so often quoted by the Imagist poets, derives from the earlier essays, "Idéalisme" and "Symbolisme," and does not add a great deal to them. It does, however, bring the rather abstract principles of the earlier discussions to bear on concrete problems of criticism. It asserts once again the principle of the "ideality of the world" and defines symbolism as the expression of individualism in art. Taking issue with Max Nordau's contention that non-conformism is an artistic sin, Gourmont maintained that, since the world exists only as the individual's personal representation of it, the capital crime of a writer must be conformism and imitativeness. The work of an artist must be not only in the reflection, but the enlarged reflection of his own personality. In a statement much admired by Ezra Pound, Gourmont maintained that, "The only excuse a man has for writing is to write himself, to reveal to others the sort of man reflected in his individual mirror; the only excuse is to be original." The critical essays in *Les Livres des Masques* are consequently devoted to isolating and evaluating elements of difference in each writer—those aspects which differentiate writers rather than relate them.

By the turn of the century, however, Gourmont had modified his views considerably. He did not so much reject his earlier opinions as try to bring them into line with newer convictions resulting from further studies of science and philology; he did not discard his idealism in favor of materialism but tried rather to see them as different aspects of the same necessary concept of reality. He did not turn his back on Symbolism, as some critics have suggested—though his later emphasis on hard, direct, concise style appears to be the exact opposite of his earlier precepts. The fact is that his works on style, which so impressed Eliot and the Imagists, are based on a sort of "physiological subjectivism" resulting from his studies of science, and are not far removed from his earlier "intellectual subjectivism." They retain the same stress on individualism and liberty and the same belief in the ultimate value of art that characterized his writings on Symbolism. What he discarded were not essential aspects of Symbolism so much as undesirable elements in himself: his *préciosité*, his excessively elaborate and refined style, his taste for the perverse and bizarre, his obsession with eroticism in all forms, his undue concern for novelty at the expense of other values, and his haughty disdain for "non-Symbolist" writers, which occasionally descended to the level of personal invective.

These rejected elements cannot, however, be dismissed as mere aberrations of immaturity. They were not peculiar to Gourmont—they belonged to the age, to the period of the 1880's and 1890's, and they were intense and exaggerated in direct proportion as they were seen as the instruments of the salvation of art. In other words, the writings of Gourmont's Symbolist period must be considered in their intellectual contexts, against the background of literary and philosophical activity which gave them birth. In reading Gourmont's defense of Symbolism, for example, one must remember the precarious position of that young movement, under fire as it was by such critical pundits as Brunetière, Anatole France, Jules Lemaître, Nordau, Lombroso, and others. The defiant gestures and belligerent tones were not confined to Gourmont or to his colleagues of the *Mercure de France,* but were shared by most writers in the small literary journals of the time.

The intellectual spirit of the period was, among the more serious writers at least, one of pessimism, stemming in part from such immediate historical events as the Franco-Prussian War and the sordid spectacles associated with the Industrial Revolution; it also derived from the ideological theories of Taine and the depressing fiction of Zola's Naturalist school, and from philosophical concepts like Schopenhauer's gloomy "Will." Science had provided no solace for the loss of faith. Furthermore, poets, and those who spoke for them, were fighting to regain their "unity of being." From the time of the "Great Schism" in the seventeenth century, man had been fragmented, divided against himself; and poets—the Symbolist poets above all—were out to make him whole again. Northrop Frye has pointed out how the Symbolists bitterly attacked contemporary contributors to the tradition of dualism and the "dissociated sensibility," and rejected the division of man and universe into arbitrary antinomies. The Enlightenment had accepted Descartes' dualism and produced men of Reason on the one hand and men of Feeling on the other, Kant had divided the world into phenomena and noumena, Schopenhauer had devised a world of Idea and a world of unconscious Will, and Dr. Charcot and his student Freud were in the process of posing a subconscious libido struggling against a censoring consciousness. The Romantics upheld the primacy of the emotions and the Realists emphasized the primacy of the objective world. One saw language as "expression" and the other thought of language as "description." It is this abyss "between noumena and phenomena and between rational knowledge (the world of perception) and poetic knowledge (the world of experience) that accounts for the emphasis which the Symbolists placed upon suggestion and evocation and for their distrust of didacticism and the 'demonstrably true.'" [6] They tried to unify the world and human experience. And so they fought vigorously all persons and ideas which seemed to further the old dichotomies. Because this spirit of revolt was concomitant with a prevailing political and social freedom, vituperative blasts against classes and individuals were common and were part of a general reaction against science and society in favor of Idealism and Art. Extreme individualism became the highest good in a struggle for freedom from a depressing determinism in the realm of philosophy and from inherited artistic principles in the realm of aesthetics. This struggle led to a spawning of "manifestoes" and artistic experiments, in which the classic distinctions between genres were threatened by the emphasis on new, extreme techniques, as represented by free verse and the Théâtre d'Art. All of which caused the fires of controversy to burn the brighter.

It was perhaps for this reason that during its early years the *Mercure de France* was not distinguished by the excellence of its criticism. Drawing its articles from such writers as Camille Mauclair, Laurent Tailhade, Jules Renard, Charles Morice, and Gourmont, it offered its readers no special program (the Symbolist emphasis came a few years later), but rather an attack upon the *status quo* of literature and upon its current leaders. It was dominated by the "anti" spirit. In the *Mercure* of 1890, these attacks took two forms: those on authors and literary movements and those on generalities like customs, institutions, and social standards.[7] The former belabored Naturalism and certain individuals—Zola, Brunetière, Rosny, Péladan, Bourget, Loti, Daudet, and Lemaître; the latter stressed materialism, the bourgeoisie, the army, and conventional morality. As an example of the personal assault then in vogue, Lawrence Bussard offers the following, from a criticism by Gourmont of Bourget's *Un Coeur de femme*: "We claim not to have understood its significance and we are completely persuaded that it does not have any." [8] Bussard concludes that "the tenor of the *Mercure* of 1890 can be summed up in one word: revolt."

But as suggested above, this virulence of tone was prompted in part by the weightiness of the opposition.

The Symbolists had formidable and influential enemies. Brunetière, for example, had started by praising Symbolism for freeing poetic expression from its bonds and for emphasizing the "soul" of phenomena lying behind appearances—as distinct from the "heavy mass of naturalism"—but he ended by disapproving of many of its works. He began, in "Le Symbolisme contemporain" (1891), with an assertion which could have been made by Gourmont: "Symbolism is the essence of poetry; indeed, symbolism pervades all of life, religion, politics—language itself is but symbolism." But he objected to the modern Symbolists' pretensions to having discovered something new—they had merely rediscovered it. Moreover, they might have had the right to seek new verse forms, whose complexity, harmony and fluidity comply with the Symbolists' conviction that those elements comprise the essence of poetry, but their search for new forms and "polymorphism" leads dangerously toward "amorphism." He also questioned their insistence on reforming the language: they did not have to "enrich" the dictionary or set traditional syntax on its head. Furthermore, it is necessary that at least one facet of a symbol be clear. A great writer in any genre is one who can clearly express even obscure ideas. It follows that modern Symbolists should renounce their habitually unintelligible style—if only to avoid the reproach that they use it to conceal the poverty of their ideas. It is easy to write unintelligibly, he added, but should their poems by chance contain something, it would be most difficult to disengage it. Symbolism is by nature universal and general, whereas the modern Symbolists are guilty of artificiality in their juxtaposition of private sensations, and of naïveté in their cultivation of emotions and banal verities—all under the pernicious example of Baudelaire. He concluded that the value of the Symbolists' critical ideas, which are admirable, is independent of the value of their actual works, which are execrable.[9]

Anatole France was equally hostile toward both the theory and practice of Symbolism. While granting that the Symbolists were no doubt sincere, he was offended

by their arrogance, their obscurity, and what he considered their excessive individualism.[10] He scolded them
for their disregard of the masses and reminded them that
language and literature are for communication and understanding and are not intended for the élite. Literature
should remain "close to life." [11] By way of opposing the
younger generation's individualism, France pointed out
that art is "collective" and owes much to the past and to
contemporaries. Language and thought are not wholly
one's own: "Let us be wise enough to recognize the
fact that our works are far from being entirely our own.
They grow in us, but their roots are everywhere in the
nourishing soil. Let us admit then that we owe much to
everyone and that the public is our collaborator." [12] Also,
"individualism developed to the point where we now see
it as a dangerous evil." [13] France granted the element of
"suggestion" as Symbolism's greatest contribution, but
found clarity more to his own taste. Furthermore, Symbolism was too neurotic; it probably would not endure, as it
was too out of step with the people.[14]

It is interesting to note that Anatole France and Remy
de Gourmont were both ironic skeptics, working, as
Burton Rascoe puts it, the same side of the street, but
with an incredible unconcern for each other. Only once
in his considerable volume of work does France mention
Gourmont—a brief review in the *Temps* of *Le Latin
mystique*, and Gourmont mentions France only a few
times. The two met twice through the efforts of their
admirers, but the relationship never prospered. France
had not only dismissed the Symbolist movement, including Gourmont, but he had displayed a "rare petti-
ness." He misspelled, apparently deliberately, Rimbaud's
name—as Raimbaud; he grouped Rimbaud with Ghil
(also misspelled) and then made out that both, and by
inference their followers Velaine and Moréas, were vic-
tims of a physical and mental malady of interest to
pathologists and that their work was of no interest. This,
coming from a man of France's renown, was indeed a
cause for battle.[15]

Like Anatole France, Jules Lemaître was out of sympathy with much contemporary literature. He also felt that the younger generation was neurotic and unduly pessimistic, showing an unhealthy concern for supernaturalism and mysticism, and infected with "a sad sensuality." [16] He disliked the Symbolists principally for their neglect of the traditional meanings of words and function of syntax. He characterized their works as "perfectly unintelligible," not only to the average reader but to the most perspicacious of cultivated people as well.[17] He objected to their use of symbols, claiming that their lack of precision and clarity was a method "suitable for poets who do not have many ideas." Symbolism wished, in his opinion, to impose on the French language certain functions at variance with its essential nature.[18]

It was against such formidable attacks as these, then, that Gourmont posed his wit, erudition, artistry, and whatever philosophical weapons he could derive from the German idealists. He fought, on the one hand, by means of critical and philosophical essays, and, on the other, by means of works of art.

The early Idealist-Symbolist philosophy of Gourmont is given dramatic form by his novels and plays. As works of imaginative literature they are not without a certain charm, deriving largely from originality of conception and deftness of style; but Gourmont lacked the power to create and animate human characters and to project them into significant and convincing situations. Perhaps he lacked the interest rather than the power, for he was concerned with working out, in what must be called novels and plays only for a lack of better terms, certain problems related to his idealistic philosophy. He says in his preface to *Le Livre de Masques*, "Literature is in fact nothing more than the artistic development of an idea by means of imaginary heroes." The early novels *Sixtine* (1890) and *Les Chevaux de Diomède* (1897), for example, can be best understood as fictional efforts to prove that the world is representation and perception is hallucination; their originality stems from the systematic way in which this idealist metaphysic is conceived in terms of character. The characters do not prove the value of the theory by their acts or words, but by their origins and their mode of existence. They exist and are explainable only because of "idealism"; they are, as Marcel Coulon puts it, "all creations of a creation," [19] the mental fabrication of one principal character who creates them, projects them from his own mind, manipulates them like marionettes, but with such dexterity that they have, or give, the same illusion of life that their creator possesses. With each main character of a novel we are present at the creation of a personal world which, according to the idealist view, is the only world.

In *Sixtine* the beautiful and enchanting heroine Sixtine Magne is seen only as the materialized sensibility of the narrator, Hubert d'Entragues, who is obviously modeled on Huysmans' Des Esseintes. He says, "I have special faculties of vision; an object about which I think very strongly appears before my eyes in a visible form, and to my tactile senses, in a palpable materiality." Being hardly capable of any joys other than the "pure joys of the mind," d'Entragues proves to his own satisfaction the vanity of physical pleasures—they are simply illusions. Furthermore, idealism gives him the means of satisfying each of his ambitions and desires, as soon as they are born, through imaginative projection. For example, when he wishes to be a Catholic Cardinal in Rome, he creates through intense mental activity all the necessary conditions, the accoutrements, the attitudes, the emotions, connected with such an experience, and he is content. "Then what good is reality to me, when I have the dream and Protean ability to transform myself, to possess successively all the forms of life, all the diverse states of the human soul?" [20]

Gourmont pushes to the extreme his demonstration of the truth that the dream gives value to life, and he follows it to its furthest consequences. As d'Entragues holds that the True is only what one believes it to be, he is convinced the "dream suffices," that "life is only a state of dream," and that "reality is thought." He is thus armed

with a contempt for physical life which renders him in-
sensible to all the deceptions to which his delicate nature
exposes him. He is completely self-sufficient, just as is
Diomède, who differs from d'Entragues only in that his
more pagan nature is not content to be focused on one
woman and who experiences a whole procession of lovely
ladies, all creations of his own fertile sensibility.

These works cannot, however, be taken completely at
their face value. While they possess the coherence and
autonomy of legitimate works of art, they are also literary
gambits in a war of ideas. They are intended to "prove"
something, to refute the materialistic basis of Naturalistic
literature, and this tendentiousness accounts to a great
extent for the extreme nature of their assertions. What
the Symbolists were opposed to in Naturalism was that it
believed so strongly in "nature" as to despise "art," and
that it loved "reality" so fervently as to scorn the "dream."
Idealism-Symbolism was out to prove that reality is
relative; that where the Naturalists saw certainty, absolute-
ness, and immutability, there was actually only possibility,
appearance, and change. The Symbolists wished to
demonstrate the invisible and true reality by the visible
representation of reality. Nevertheless, after having
drawn from the principle of the ideality of the world all
that it can give to liberate the creative imagination and
aesthetic judgment, and after having supported the rights
of the dream, the imagination, the ideal, Gourmont will
admit—in fact will proclaim—that in practice external
reality does exist. From one point of view, *Sixtine* can be
considered a criticism as well as an apology for extreme
idealism and negation of action, for while the main
characters affirm the necessity and virtue of the idealist
position, it is the limits and dangers that are actually being
demonstrated. The conclusions of *Sixtine* and *Les
Chevaux de Diomède* show that imagination can replace
action only to a certain extent. Throughout these novels
Gourmont demonstrates, despite the seeming emphasis
on idealism, that there is an important difference between
the woman of flesh and blood, for example, and the

woman of dreams, between the idea and the object, between the intellectual conception of life and that life itself.

A similar modification of Idealism was made in the essay "Dernière Conséquence de l'Idéalisme," *La Culture des Idées* (1894). This work reviewed the conclusions of earlier statements on Idealism and confessed a few doubts as to the "consequences" of extreme subjectivism. Using the figures of Narcissus and Dante's Ugolino as symbols, Gourmont made a case for "a life of relationship." He did not refute the subjectivist position but emphasized that one can live in and by one's own thoughts only as they are nourished from the external world, whose existence must be granted, however illusory that world may be and however dependent it may be upon our thoughts for its existence. For the thinking mind is equally dependent upon that world for its own existence. Otherwise it would die, just as Ugolino is condemned to death for eating, in enforced solitude, his own children (i.e., thoughts), and Narcissus, having lost his Echo, must perish. That is, "for the limited intelligence, the conditions of thought are completely different; it needs the stimulus of external shock. Reduced to itself, the intelligence is a prisoner in solitary confinement. In that situation, thought absorbs itself and is dissolved into non-thought." Thus Gourmont took another step towards coming to terms with the physical world. The last step was taken in an essay written in 1904, after the publication of *Physique de l'Amour*, and was based on Gourmont's interim study of zoology.

In this essay, "Les Racines de l'Idéalisme," [21] Gourmont retracted his earlier criticism in Lamarck (in *Physique de l'Amour*), who held that "the milieu creates the organ." Gourmont now agreed, but he showed how this concept leads back to a belief in Idealism, to which he always remained faithful. He admitted that the sense organs are created and formed in response to external stimuli—the milieu—and that the organs must correspond to external realities, for they are not created by the perceiving organism but by the perceived environment. As these senses must correspond to the "externals" which created them, those externals are not a dream, or an illusion, but a reality pre-existent to the organ that perceives them, and independent of it. Visible objects in the milieu must be perceived by the eye in the form of an exact image, since the eye is the very work of that luminous milieu.

Gourmont also advanced the theory that there is a "physique de la pensée," that thought is not only a "product" but is material, measurable, and ponderable. Thought is a result, a consequence, a property of the nervous system or even of living matter. It is unthinkable that it should be isolated from the causes which produce it.

Thought is a product but it is also productive. It does not create the world, but it judges it; it does not destroy the world, but modifies it and reduces it to its own measure. To know is to bring a judgment and all judgment is arbitrary, both because it is an adaptation, a mean derived from sense experiences, and because two different physiologies give different means or averages, just as they give different extremes. This leads one back to subjective idealism again. Idealism is thus founded on the very materialism of thought, considered as a physiological product.

Furthermore, the conception of the external world as knowable is compatible only with a belief in the existence of an infallible reason, or soul—an immutable, incorruptible principle of knowing. But if knowledge of externals is the work of thought, which is a humble physiological product differing in quality and mode from man to man, from species to species, then the world can be considered as unknowable, since each brain or each nervous system draws from its vision and sensations a different image. Even if received sensations were at first same for all, the world would yet be profoundly modified in its final representation by the intervention of individual judgment.

The apparent results of Gourmont's philosophical revisions were that he, and those who shared his views and who had started out with great hopes of what the newly imported German philosophy would do for art, soon fell back on less ambitious kinds of interpretations. For, ultimately, all that Gourmont and his associates meant to say was that "perceptions, as accounted for by a realist epistomology, are subject to distortion when they are subjected to processes of an affective nature." [22] And this is all that Gourmont had in mind when, a few years later, examining at length the implications of the Schopenhauer doctrines he had praised in the earlier *Livres des Masques*, he concluded that not only is idealism based squarely on "the very materialism of thought, considered as a physiological product," but moreover that the roots of idealism are planted deep in the material world and, conversely, materialism really means idealism.[23]

This philosophy, it must be noted, did not hinder Gourmont in his own studies of external phenomena. He examined nature closely and even erected "laws" on the basis of those examinations. Nowhere in his scientific writings does the suggestion creep in that his findings, and those of his masters Ribot, Quinton, and Fabre, might not hold for all men and all nature. But whenever philosophizing on the subject of science, he admitted that all scientific discoveries are highly hypothetical and provisional.

The important point here, for the purposes of this study, is that Gourmont based his very influential early writings about aesthetics, criticism, and style squarely on a subjective idealism progressively modified by an acceptance of the existence and importance of external phenomena. It is evident, however, that most of Gourmont's Anglo-American disciples were impressed more by his emphatic statements on liberty and by the example of his own practice than by the intellectual concepts on which they were founded. The extreme subjectivism of Gourmont during the early period of his life could not have appealed to the Imagist poets, to whom the external world not only existed but was to be described in as direct, precise, and concrete fashion as possible. To Ezra Pound the natural object was always the "adequate symbol," and he did not question the poet's ability to apprehend it. The early Gourmont, then, served as an inspiring example in the war against bourgeois morality and mediocrity in art, but it was the later Gourmont whose writings on science, philology, and literary criticism furnished most of the theories and epigraphs so freely borrowed by English and American writers.

ii

On the whole, it was not the theories, the great scientific constructions, that appealed to Gourmont, but rather the "facts of life" that those theories taught him. He felt that scientific curiosity and the eternal search for ideas and facts should give one intoxicating momentary sensations of possession: "one could reconstruct the world on sensation." In these moments of "internal consent," one understood oneself, grasped the mystery, and embraced life:

> We need a one-floor philosophy, familiar and scientific, always subject to new facts which necessarily arise, a philosophy which may be only a commentary on life, but on the whole of life. Man separated from the rest of nature is a pure mystery. In order to comprehend something for ourselves, we must cast ourselves, humbly, back into the vital milieu whence religious pride has dragged us in order to elevate us to the dignity of puppets of the ideal. There is now but one philosophy worthy of the name: scientific philosophy.[24]

Thus we see that by 1905 the idealism of Gourmont was of a purely terrestrial origin. He did not seek chimerical "motifs d'exaltation" in the negation of life, as did his early master Villiers de l'Isle-Adam. The sensual and mystical impulses of his mind now sprang from the experiences of daily life. Mysticism, he said, speaking of

Maeterlinck, "makes no appeal except to that infinity which resides in us and in which we believe in proportion as we live and meditate. . . . I seek, with Maeterlinck . . . 'possibility of superior life in the humble and inevitable daily reality.' " [25]

Gourmont wanted to discover a "scientific" philosophy of art. Like many of his generation, he suffered from the conflict between intelligence, which wished to embrace the universe, and a highly refined sensibility, which pulled the mind toward flesh and matter. Even while glorifying the intellect, Gourmont was at pains to reveal its mechanisms and to lay bare the naked and natural animal behind the mask of man's smug superiority. Even in his extreme "cerebrality," he was always aware, and insisted that his readers be aware, of the dominance of the physical life.

Gourmont believed that Christian morality, by setting man apart from nature, had, in the name of his supposed superiority, also set him apart from the full realization of his physical life. Such a morality imposes on man a strict abnegation in its proclaiming that he, the most perfect of beings, is the crowning achievement of creation, and that freedom of the will permits him to dominate his animal inclinations, especially his sexual instincts. Gourmont's morality, on the other hand, was based on the full activity of all the senses, a principle opposite to that of abnegation. This morality, derived mainly from Gourmont's own nature, recognized but one law, the tyranny of the nervous system, and but one restraint, the individual conscience.[26] There are no moral sensations or ideas, but only moral feelings. Sensations are the *facts*, and should be studied freely. But feelings, or emotions, must be examined from a moral point of view, because they are motives of action, and the only possible justification for concern with morality, which is usually indifferent to ideas and sensations, is that action must not be anti-social. This is the only limit that Gourmont gave to individual liberty. But within those limits, his morality proclaimed that the individual should know all the pleasure available to man, for we have but one life, the earthly one.[27]

To support these views Gourmont drew upon the philosophy of Epicurus, whose ideas, Gourmont believed, were prophetic of the results of contemporary research and experience. The atomic theory, the laws of selection and heredity, the principles of positive psychology, our aspirations to intellectual freedom—all were presaged in the Epicurean system. For the same reasons we must also admit Epicurus' morality:

> The principle of that morality is not duty—an idea the Christians borrowed, without really understanding it, from the Stoics; it is pleasure. Let us not understand by that word anything too gross or too subtle. The pleasure of living, of enjoying all the conscious or unconscious activities to which we lend our bodies. To disdain the body in order to exalt who knows what spiritual principle which could only have its own roots in that same body—such a mad idea never occurred to Epicurus.[28]

Gourmont's "happiness" is a physical condition balanced by intelligence and sensibility, which in turn multiplied pleasure, with skepticism assuring a liberty of mind beyond the reach of conscience (a learned thing). The Good, as well as the True, is determined by our senses: what is good and moral is what is pleasant for us and serves the needs of our present sensibility.[29] For life, according to Gourmont, is a series of sensations bound together by states of consciousness. The sensations are the only facts, the only truths, and they can be evaluated by only one guiding principle—utility. Truth and utility coincide if they conform to the individual physiology, and they may agree with the truths of other people when the needs and objectives are the same.[30]

The "immoralism" of Gourmont's views derived largely from his own temperament but were given philosophical justification through his "cult of nature." Gourmont, as a disciple of Epicurus, Lucretius, and Nietzsche, was a pagan, a believer in a sort of "sensual pantheism." His writings are devoted to expounding this paganism in the service of a higher "civilization." While not averse to shocking orthodox minds, Gourmont's principal aim was to liberate, to free man mentally and physically from what he felt to be the unnatural and unhealthy constraints imposed by conventional religion and morality. He believed that civilization was the result of the most refined free play of the mind amid the riches of art and "the plenitude of the carnal life." This plenitude is based on the rights of the body, of voluptuousness, the unrestricted cultivation of sensation necessary to the fullest development of the human organism. Civilization, to Gourmont, is the cultivation of everything which Christianity calls vice, frivolity, pleasures, games, temporal business, "this world's goods," and so on. He advised against excess and any sort of depravity, and in favor of an Epicurean moderation; but to him moderation meant equilibrium, and in his opinion modern society is decidedly out of balance, a full half—perhaps the more important half—of man's nature being cramped miserably within the confines of a narrow morality.

This "immoralism" was not the negation of all moral discipline, however, but only of a universal, standardized moral law. Gourmont would have agreed with Blake's dictum, "One law for the Lion and Ox is oppression." Each must forge his own rules for living in accordance with his own sensibility, with the "psychological imperative." Gourmont, like Epicurus, was out to free man, not from fear of death and interfering gods but from the modern fear of "the ineluctable fact, the immutable law." He wanted to exorcise these spectres, and to clear the way for a philosophy which admitted nothing more absolute than life and the sensibility of living beings; for any reasonable theory of truth must be based on life, on man's essentially animal nature, on its usefulness to that animal life. Things out of relation to our senses are of little significance or value.

To this end Gourmont, in his war on religion and religion-inspired morality, brought science to bear, depriving man of his assigned place of honor in nature and showing that he is not at the summit of the universe but merely an "accident" of creation. In all his writings on science, Gourmont intended to put man back into "le milieu vital," stripped of his pride and his sovereignty. Gourmont was not out to degrade man but to exalt him: "What is most beautiful in man is his animality." As man is only one of the animals, he can fulfill his life potential only in complete awareness of his origins. If he is aware and knows his place in nature, man's conception of life will have a unity that is lacking in metaphysical systems. He will be on good terms with all his desires and sensations. In studying the life of nature, he will better understand his own life and its relationship to the rest of the animal world. Perceiving both differences and similarities between himself and other animals, he will learn to value the gifts of his most distinguishing feature, his intelligence.[31] Thus, while not abandoning his philosophical masters, Schopenhauer, Nietzsche, and Epicurus, he turned increasingly to the study of the natural sciences, zoology in particular.

Early in 1904, Gourmont, along with Edouard Dujardin, Arnold Van Gennep, and Jules de Gaultier, founded *La Revue des Idées*. With Gourmont as its editor, the review was intended to "build a bridge" between literature and science. The group centered around Dr. René Quinton, a noted zoologist who had formulated the influential theory that animals tend to conserve the body temperature given them at the time of their appearance on earth. In formulating this theory, Quinton had qualified Darwin's theories of evolution and had made a distinction between the evolution of anatomy and that of physiology: only forms (i.e., anatomies) change; physiology remains constant. Life endeavors to resist change; external circumstances force anatomical adaptations, but physiology persists. This applies only to vertebrates, however, for the invertebrates tend to change physiology, i.e., temperature and saline concentration, with external conditions. Thus in Quinton's law *fixity* dominates evolution. Fixity is the principle, evolution is the corollary; animal life tends to maintain the conditions of its origins.

Seeing in this theory a justification of his own predilections, Gourmont drew an analogy in support of his own anarchism, a rule for "superior living": one must rebel against the influence of the milieu in order to maintain one's original personality, and therefore the non-conformism of the "vertebrates" takes on a philosophical as well as biological value.

But there is a problem here, a basic contradiction which Gourmont did not fully resolve, for Gourmont, the champion of liberty and advocate of resistance to the milieu, was fundamentally a determinist. In his studies of science he came to accept the law of causality. This law was not only one of the finest conquests of the intelligence, but was the intelligence becoming conscious of itself and personifying itself,[32] a belief derived from the primary element in his materialist philosophy, the material nature of thought—thought as a product of the physiology. Like Taine before him, Gourmont claimed that there is a *sensation* at the base of each idea: "Man is a sensibility. The intelligence is only the sensibility detached from its roots and on its way to perishing, like cut flowers when one does not renew the water in the vase." [33] And the water in the vase is concrete sensation, the "shock of external excitation" which Gourmont discussed in his "Dernière Conséquence de l'Idéalisme." Style, ideas, attitudes, decisions—all are a product of the sensibility, of the total physiology, and are subject to what Gourmont called "the tyranny of the nervous system." Although Gourmont firmly believed that all of our ideas and actions are causally related and determined by our physiology, he also believed that an illusion of liberty is necessary to life.[34] Total freedom of the will is an illusion, but a certain limited measure of choice is nevertheless possible. Determining motives vary in force at different times, thus creating an element of variety in the possibilities allowing of limited selection. In *Physique de l'Amour* he said,

The belief in liberty is born of the diversity of human aptitudes, of the power man possesses to achieve by all sorts of different routes the necessary end of his activity or to elude that end and to destroy in himself the species whose future he bears. Liberty is an illusion difficult not to have, and an idea one must discard if one is to think rationally: the variety of possible human actions simulates liberty and, in practice, has almost the same results.[35]

Man is "freer" than the other animals only because his greater intelligence and more complex structure create a greater number of needs or motives and a greater number of ways to satisfy them. There is a certain freedom where there is intelligence and complexity, but in this respect man's liberty does not differ from the rest of the animate universe in kind or in quality, but only in quantity, in the number of possible directions in which he can be "determined." In his writings on individualism and liberty, therefore, Gourmont was advocating that man recognize his subservience to his nervous system. He should find or create his own "truths" in conformity with demands of his animal nature rather than try to accept the ready-made truths of society, the milieu. For it is only by living in harmony with his animal needs that man can achieve happiness or satisfaction. It is at this point that Gourmont's concept of the relativity and subjectivity of truth joins forces with his deterministic materialism. If determinism establishes the interdependence of all things, subjective idealism establishes the dependence of things "in relation to ourselves." Thus the indissoluble union of materialistic determinism and subjective idealism forms the foundation of Gourmont's conception of liberty as it is manifested in human activity.

This philosophy of determinism and "animalism" is clearly not intended to be pessimistic, neither to debase man nor to over-simplify him. Man's true nobility stems from his being a part of nature and being himself in the world of phenomena. He is the product of his own works, and has achieved supremacy by his own means and not by having profited from the "advantages of birth," divine or otherwise. While Gourmont believed man's intelligence to be an "accident" of nature, he credited it with having made possible man's present degree of freedom, and he looked to it to make possible an even greater degree in the future. And it is to this end—more freedom for the individual, be it illusion or fact—that Gourmont was always striving. For whatever his immediate objective in writing an essay or book, his ultimate goal was extension of the range of possibilities for man, and increase of sources of pleasure and satisfaction. In this sense, the materialist Gourmont was basically a moralist, for he was concerned with the conduct of life as well as the production of art.[36]

Gourmont's writings on scientific sociology, as might be expected, stirred up considerable controversy as to the validity of both his methods and findings. For example, Havelock Ellis observed, "In science and in philosophy he is the heroic amateur, lacking in training and in equipment, but never failing in keen penetration." Regarding specifically the *Physique de l'Amour*, Ellis said, "The treatment of such a subject by one who had no training in biology could scarcely be altogether adequate; Gourmont's discussion is too individual for a scientific topic, but his penetrating sagacity, wide knowledge, and daring frankness of presentation still render this a notable book." [37]

We can agree with Havelock Ellis regarding Gourmont's erudition and daring, and still have reservations about the validity of his scientific books. Gourmont's conclusions are often fascinating, sometimes convincing, but they are nevertheless rendered dubious by the author's methods. One senses that he is not being truly objective in his "scientific" researches. Gourmont had definite points to prove and a thesis to maintain, which were clearly formulated before he began his studies, and hence the evidence falls neatly into place. The *Physique de l'Amour*, like his other works of erudition, is a pleasure to read for its style and wealth of information on the animal world, and it may also be read for its analogies and "principles," which are unfailingly provocative. But because Gourmont, in his zeal to prove the absurdity of society's sexual conventions, was inclined to draw rather heady generalizations from a very small basis of fact, he is often more stimulating than reliable.

The accuracy of Gourmont's science, however, I leave for experts to judge. It is sufficient for my purposes to demonstrate that Gourmont's aesthetic beliefs, as well as his ethics, rested squarely on his philosophy of nature. He was convinced that thought is a product of the sensibility; he emphasized the close connections which unite intelligence to sensibility and consequently to the body; and he gave a predominant role to the brain in the assimilation of sensations and in the birth of ideas. These convictions did not mean, however, that Gourmont was in accord with the many psychological critics of the day who would explain an author's works entirely in terms of his physiology (i.e., genius as the result of insanity, the malfunctioning of organs, etc.). Although such studies might have a general and theoretical interest, he considered them to be without value in the explication of the work of an individual author. Just as he rejected many of Sainte-Beuve's psychological analyses, so he doubted that the mysteries of individual creation could be solved by medical or psychiatric investigation. The superior man, the artist, escaped all such explanations.[38]

The important thing here is that Gourmont's attention was continually drawn to what he considered the essential problem: the role of physiology in artistic creation. He was to devote much thought to this problem, so central to much of his critical writing. He wanted to know how sensation was transformed into inspiration, how intelligence achieved a work of art. To accomplish this, Gourmont was obliged somehow to reconcile his materialistic theories with the intellectualist theories inherited from Mallarmé, who had maintained that, in effect, the initial sensation in a creative process could be consciously and voluntarily provoked by the poet himself, thanks to the power of the Word.[39] Once the sensation had registered, the poet's

intelligence proceeded to strip the sensation of its concrete elements, leaving only the pure idea, *la notion pure*.
For Gourmont, however, the essence lay not in an abstracted idea. On the contrary, it remained in the sensation, the "vital tremor"; and, in addition to the sensation
and the intervention of the intellect, there was a long and
mysterious process, the transformation of the initial sensation in the unconscious. For Gourmont the inexplicable
power of the unconscious (or subconscious) is the true
creator of a work of art: "Consciousness, which is the
principle of liberty, is not the principle of art." Far from
being tied to the functioning of consciousness, intellectual
activity is most often disturbed by it, for the subconscious
is the source of real thought and therefore of inspiration.
We are not thinking when we know we are thinking:
"One thinks badly when one knows that one thinks:
consciousness of thinking is not thought." [40]

Here Gourmont was facing up to one of the main
problems that arose during his time and that still challenges aestheticians today: the role of the subconscious
in the creative process. In "La Création subconsciente"
(*La Culture des Idées*) he argued that we cannot summon
"inspiration" whenever we wish; that the poet, no less
than the scientist, must wait until the form or solution of a
problem offers itself, seemingly of its own accord, to the
thinking mind.

> Imaginative intellectual creation is inseparable from the
> frequency of the subconscious state, and in this category of
> creations must be included the discovery of the scientist
> and the ideological constructions of the philosopher. All
> who have invented or discovered something new in any field
> whatsoever, are men of imagination as well as observers.
> The most deliberate, the most thoughtful, the most pains-
> taking writer is constantly, and in spite of himself, enriched
> by the effort of the subconscious. No sentence, perhaps,
> however worked over, was ever spoken or written in abso-
> lute accord with the will. The search for the right word in
> the vast, deep reservoir of verbal money is itself an act
> which escapes so completely from the control of the will,

that very often the word on its way flees at the very moment when consciousness is about to perceive and to grasp it.

Gourmont was not suggesting that automatism is the sole condition of creative activity. He was emphasizing his belief that, in his search for an adequate embodiment of a feeling, the artist cannot rely on solutions, or inferences from solutions, of other artistic problems. Each problem is unique; no two are alike; each must be solved in its own way. It is in this sense that Gourmont thought that consciousness, the reasoning intellect, fails the artist. Therefore, the artist, at any crucial moment in the creative process, falls back on his more fundamental faculties.

In response to critics who deplored this down-grading of the conscious mental processes,[41] Gourmont insisted that the intelligence is the organ of criticism, not of creation: "Intelligence serves to criticize our acts, not to determine them." In the process of creation, the intelligence is only a "timid counsellor." The force which creates escapes the control of consciousness. However, Gourmont concedes that the conscious intellect might serve as a collaborator of the subconscious; that is, the intellect might watch over its subjacent activities while the initial sensations are being transformed into a work of art, which surveillance suffices to distinguish true inspiration from delirium and dream. Furthermore, as he said of Sir Isaac Newton's creative activity, "In Newton's case (as a result of constant attention) the work of the subconscious is continuous, but connects itself periodically with voluntary activity. Now conscious, now unconscious, his thought explores all activities." But Gourmont warns that the conscious intellect, if it interferes at the wrong time and in the wrong way, can damage and even destroy the originality, vitality, and even the sincerity of the subconscious creation.

Right or wrong, Gourmont's ideas on the subconscious and the creative process were derived from an extensive study of contemporary French and German psychology. The French psychologists of the nineteenth century emphasized the new science of psychiatry. Associationism and physiological psychology had found an able exponent in Taine (*De l'Intelligence*), but psychiatry continued to be the area where the French made their greatest contributions. Men like Richet and Freud's master, Charcot, stressed the unconscious and the possibilities of hypnosis, and Charcot's student, Janet, was interested in the process of dissociation, the splitting of personality. The dominant figure of the time, however, often cited by Gourmont as a source, was Théodule Ribot, whose *L'Imagination créatrice* (1900) Gourmont found especially stimulating. Ribot represented the fusion of two streams of psychological investigation—psychiatric practice and mechanistic theory—and saw brain physiology as the basis of personality. Ribot, along with William James, Alfred Binet, Féré, and others, emphasized physiological functions as important clues of psychological functions, and developed a new psychology dependent on the findings of physiological research.

The discoveries of these men provided the "scientific" foundations of Gourmont's psychosomatic concept of the human organism and his belief in the deterministic relationship between the subconscious and the creative process. But it was to Dr. Paul Chabaneix's *Physiologie cérébrale: le subconscient chez les artistes, les savants, et les écrivains* that Gourmont was chiefly indebted in his own "La Création Subconsciente." This essay was in fact written "à propos" of Chabaneix's work, as Gourmont explained in a footnote. He discussed Chabaneix's belief that in the process of artistic creation the initial sensation is transformed according to the laws of a rigorous determinism. Sensation enters the subconscious, where it is received and modified by preceding elements, and where it in turn joins with those elements to receive and modify following sensations. Inspiration is therefore a chain of associations of sensations, of which each link is evoked and determined by the preceding link. The intervention of consciousness is harmful, according to Chabaneix, if it happens before this inspirational process is finished, because the consciousness has the power, as Gourmont put it, "to modify the deterministic logic, to break the series of associations in order to create voluntarily in the mind the first link in a new chain." [42]

Eugène Bencze makes the interesting observation that Gourmont's ideas on the mental processes are at once more mystical and more scientific than those of the other Symbolists, especially those of Mallarmé, whose work seems to be done in the bright light of the conscious intellect.[43] Mallarmé believed that the activities of the poet are voluntary—from the initial provocation of sensation to the choice of expression; and his follower Valéry said that once in a while a first line might come as the "gift of the gods," but that the rest of a poem was a matter of conscious effort.

It is interesting to compare Gourmont's ideas with the theory of the creative process elaborated by Valéry in his writings on the genius of Leonardo da Vinci. Valéry believed that by a prolonged and rigorous study of one's mental processes, a superior intellect may in time acquire the power to distinguish its center of consciousness from its habitual "encrustations" of personality. The mind can become a "suspended point of total awareness" to which all things, whether of one's own being (sensation, emotions, etc.), or of the external world, become observable and "equal" as separate entities, independent of one's mind yet susceptible of being manipulated into new and original structures.

A principal difference between this view and that of Gourmont is of course that Gourmont would allow the intellect a lesser role in the "manipulation" of its material. Indeed, Gourmont reversed the order of causality established by other Symbolists and asserted that it is not the will which places the artist in the center of a network of stimuli, to register sensations voluntarily evoked or consciously sought. Sensation is the principal condition of creation, because it activates the intellect and consequently the will. Gourmont granted that the individual cannot be fully explained by physiology, but he also affirmed that, thanks to the teachings of this science, a general explanation and theory of creation is possible. As Bencze points out, on the one hand there is the mystery of inspiration, but on the other hand there is sensation, the point of departure of Gourmont's entire philosophy and one stable principle in his network of ideas and arguments. Mystery and sensation, the two fixed points, also determine his criticism. In deference to the mystery, he would "remake his aesthetic" for each individual and each work, but he demanded of each work that it be born of concrete sensation, the only criterion of truth and sincerity. These are the principles on which Gourmont founded his "impressionistic" theories of literary criticism; and in his essays his practice of criticism is consistent with his physiological and sensualist theories.

It should be added, however, that Gourmont's theories posed a difficult problem of which he was well aware. The marriage of the two "infinites," mystery and sensation, is not invariably a happy one. The incessant struggle between sensibility and intelligence appeared to Gourmont to be the essence of all animal life, a struggle in which the intelligence destroys physical pleasures after having enjoyed them only for a fleeting moment. Drawing in part from the ideas of Schopenhauer and from the French philosopher Jules de Gaultier, but working primarily out of his own acute self-awareness, Gourmont suggested that sensation is transformed into intelligence, but that when the metamorphosis kills pleasure, one experiences a sense of loss. Carried to the symbolic plane, the regrets of a moment become a source of universal sadness; and Gourmont posed the principle that "the intelligence, in supplanting sensation, kills life. The instinct for knowledge kills the instinct for life."

Gourmont was well aware of the underlying cause of his own disquietude. In an essay on "Art and Science" (1902), he described the nature of science: "It is life devouring itself, it is the sensibility being transformed into intelligence, it is the need to know stifling the need to live, it is the genius of knowledge vivisecting the vital genius."

This view of the role of science in human life creates for Gourmont a dilemma which he was unable to resolve, but he would probably respond that he did not resolve it because it is unresolvable—it is the eternal human condition.[44] For although he believed that in the creative artist intelligence is but an aspect, a development, of the sensibility, he observed in the case of objective science a dissociation of sensibility from the intelligence that was to divide man's nature into two contending camps. In fact, it was Gourmont's acute awareness of the perpetual struggle between those contending forces of man's nature, between the often conflicting demands of the reason and the sensibility, that gave interest, vitality, and profundity to his own best work.

iii

While it is possible to piece together a reasonably clear picture of his aesthetic theories, Gourmont's views on society and politics resolutely resist schematization. He was opposed to theories and formulas and considered a state of contradiction as the most favorable atmosphere for the free functioning of the mind. He presented no program, for he was not interested in proselytizing. He did not believe in collective happiness but was convinced that each individual must work out his own philosophy and his own salvation, independent of theories and systems.

He was, however, quite clear in what he opposed: democracy, capitalism, communism, socialism, even parliamentarianism. Politically he seemed to be some kind of aristocratic anarchist. He sneered at the idea of progress and was very bitter on the subject of the French Revolution. He denied religious optimism but, perhaps because of the influence of Nietzsche, refused to embrace its usual alternative, humanitarian optimism. Universal disarmament and peace he found to be historically and scientifically unfeasible. Opposed to any kind of United States of Europe, he maintained that each nation should, like an individual, cultivate its own personality, for interesting relations among nations depend on their originality and pride. The relative interest of each human type, whether individual or national, lies in those qualities which the others do not possess. Hence Gourmont's emphasis, especially in his *Esthétique de la Langue française,* on retaining purity of language as the basis of a sense of nationality.

Gourmont's philosophy was founded on a basically anti-social individualism, strongly oriented toward Nietzsche's "superman" but qualified by two important character-istics: a highly developed sense of fact, and what Garnet Rees calls Gourmont's "instrument de maître," his skepti-cism. His sense of fact led him to the study of science, for he wanted to dominate emotions and ideas, to view the world with the detachment of an entomologist and to remain outside of all preconceptions in order to leave his mind free to follow without hindrance the evolutions of its thought. As a result of this extreme desire for an un-committed intellect, free to move and choose sides at will, Gourmont's ideas, as noted by many of his critics, are a mass of apparent contradictions. For example, he was an atheist with a great interest in the Catholic Church and an admiration for many of its saints; he stressed the unimportance of humanity while defending the impor-tance of the individual man; he considered the human intellect an "accident" or "error" in the scheme of things, yet praised the beauty of the perfectly functioning mind; he saw man both as an animal and as something quite distinct from all animals; he was intellectually a pessimist, but temperamentally an optimist; basically an aristocrat, he was however not completely anti-democratic—if any-thing, he was an anarchist; he modeled himself on eight-eenth-century writers, but was hostile to rationalism; he exalted "civilization" but hated everything that placed restraints on the instincts; he was fundamentally a tra-ditionalist, but loved originality and novelty; he was at-tracted by science, while retaining his passion for art; he was a scientific determinist who wrote vigorous articles in defense of individual freedom; he was an avowed materialist whose major efforts were expended on behalf of idealism; and he tied all these contradictory attitudes together by means of a subtle logic. His life was dedicated, one might say, to the resolution and synthesis of these ideas.

It was in this atmosphere of contradiction that Gourmont felt most comfortable. He believed, along with the early Ezra Pound, that intellectual conviction meant intellectual death: "Philosophically, I consider contradiction as necessary to intellectual and emotional equilibrium. Without it, one would fall into mania and from mania into conviction, which is the last degree of stupidity." [45] The terms "faith" and "certainty" were to Gourmont only objects of ridicule and scorn.

Because of this skepticism Gourmont in many ways resembles the eighteenth-century *philosophes*. One can find analogies between his "dissociation of ideas" and Bayle's *Dictionnaire historique et critique* and between the dialogue on liberty in Voltaire's *Dictionnaire philosophique* and Gourmont's *Physique de l'Amour*.[46] There is little doubt that if the *philosophes* did not influence Gourmont's ideas, they at least conditioned his attitudes. In manner of expression and point of view, he was very close to the spirit of the Encyclopedists. But as a matter of fact, Gourmont did not read the eighteenth-century *philosophes* with sympathy until late in life, and in 1904 we find that he actually detested Voltaire. In both *Le Problème du Style* (1902) and an article written in 1904 Voltaire is included among the examples of bad writers, the "banal type of abstract writer." [47] By 1907, however, Gourmont had changed his mind. In his *Dialogues des Amateurs* a character (who represents Gourmont's views) says, "I like a mind to be diverse, and that is what makes me so admire Voltaire, whose greatness I have finally come to understand." Thus Gourmont had come to admire Voltaire for his diversity of interests, his intellectual freedom, and his method of attack—raillery. Voltaire had become a cherished precursor.

Gourmont's relations with Renan were similar to those

with Voltaire. In 1890, during his symbolist and idealist period, he called Renan "the sinister dilettante," "the eminent professor of falsehoods," and so on. At that time Gourmont's "instrument de maître" was not yet in hand; he was engaged, rather unskeptically, in the battle for Idealism-Symbolism. But it was through his study of idealism that Gourmont came to adopt the principle of skepticism: Since the world is representation and dependent on the data given by the senses, diversity of opinion is inevitable and the notion of general truth is inane. "Outside of the exact sciences, which are affirmations or explications of the principle of identity, nothing is true or false except according to the need we have for it, since nothing is comparable." [48]

In the same year he wrote a spirited defense of Renan entitled "Renan et l'Idée scientifique." [49] Brunetière had praised Renan for his style alone; Gourmont, claiming that style is inseparable from the thought it contains, defended Renan's cool skeptical rationalism and scientific mode against disparagers who doubted the power of science to probe truth. Renan, like Gourmont, was engaged in demolishing cherished Verities, and to this end he used science mainly as an instrument of negation. Thus Gourmont, who also approved of Renan's denial of progress and religious optimism, came to view Renan as an ally in his war on the principle folly of mankind: "The horrible mania for certitude."

It is quite typical of Gourmont, however, that after having vigorously expounded one point of view he should treat the opposite view with equal justice. Just as his passion for liberty was qualified by studies in determinism and his emphasis on originality was balanced by later concessions to tradition, so his admiration for skepticism was rounded out by an awareness of the possibility of duplicity and fraud. In an essay on Jules Lemaître, for example, he said that "this skepticism by an excessive aptitude for feeling is rather rare: there are others, less estimable," and he proceeded to analyze various kinds—skepticism resulting from laziness, timidity, or excessive prudence, from irresponsibility or duplicity. "The state of skepticism is so attractive that it has always made the common man envious; it cloaks his vices and failings; the hypocrisy of skepticism is one of the most wide-spread and most difficult to unmask." In certain persons, however, an honest skepticism is inevitable. They are persons whose sensibilities are pushed in different directions by contrary tendencies: "These 'contrarities' or contrary tendencies, when they are very numerous and very marked, in a conscious sensibility, necessarily engender skepticism." [50] It is this form of skepticism which Gourmont considers so rare, though doubtless possessed by Renan and himself.

An extreme example of Gourmont's skepticism is found in *Une Nuit au Luxembourg*. A certain god-like "stranger," known simply as He, after having explained the functioning of the universe and the destinies of gods and men, concludes his discourse in this way:

HE—I still have a few words to say to you, and they are the most important. You must forget our conversation.

I—Master, that is impossible. It is a part of me, it has entered into my flesh, into my blood, into my bones.

HE—Well, you should know then that I could have told you the contrary, and it would also have been the truth.[51]

What then, according to Gourmont, is "the truth?" He gives us one clear statement, the familiar position of the subjective idealist:

What is truth? Our Savior Jesus Christ, who claimed to know all things, did not know that. We are better informed today. We are no longer unaware that truth is a convenient word, composed (in French) of six letters, by which one expresses agreement between the object and the representation, that is to say, nothing which might have a meaning accessible to the human intelligence, since we never know an object, whatever its nature, except according to the mental representation we give ourselves of that object. The object has no more real existence in the representation than a tree in a photograph; and nevertheless, we must be content with the representation, for we will never see the tree, we will never see the object, we will never know if there is any concurrence, or of what kind, between what is and what we know.[52]

Further on, Gourmont says, "Truth is doubt 'tempered by contempt,' " and elsewhere, "It is as absurd to seek the truth and to find it, when one has reached the age of reason, as to put one's shoes before the fireplace on Christmas Eve." [53] But Gourmont knew that men have need of a faith—as a staff or a crutch, and he saw a new cult rising which was to him as absurd and tyrannical as its out-moded predecessors. Science, in reaching the people, reached them in the only form it might adopt if it were to penetrate so many minds: the form of a Belief. The words Science, Progress, and Evolution had been given a quasi-miraculous power. Against this new idol which had subjected so many minds and against its numerous convinced apostles, Gourmont pitted his talent for critical analysis and negative polemic. He fought against this "rationalist despotism, even more dangerous than theological despotism because of the mask of intellectual illusion with which it adorns itself in order to seduce simple and straightforward minds." [54] He saw this worship of rationalism as similar in its essentials to earlier worship of religion: "What constitutes the religious phenomenon is not the belief in a religion, but rather the belief in all truth." [55]

Gourmont places a strong emphasis on the distinction between science's *provisional* acceptance of temporary "truths" and the credulous readiness to accept all of science's findings as the last word, immutable and absolute. One of Gourmont's admirers remarks, "As a matter of fact, one of the glories of M. de Gourmont, to informed minds, was that of being able to distinguish the scientist from the hierophant, of having rendered to M. Berthelot, for example, the homage which he merited as chemist and at the same time having shown the vanity

of his philosophical visions." [56] For Gourmont was not one
to construct a philosophy; his interests lay elsewhere. His
task was to undermine "truths," not to create them.
"My business is to sow doubts. This phrase of Pierre Bayle
contains an entire method and an entire morality. Truth is
tyrannous, doubt is liberating." As an avowed individual-
ist, Gourmont wished to remain free, to avoid all certi-
tudes and above all to escape that "horrible mania for
certitude." Hence he offers not a system but a method by
which one could unmask and destroy established beliefs.
This method was his well known "dissociation of ideas."

Gourmont's thought was based on one main idea. For
him the greatest danger to human intelligence, not only to
an intelligence cut off from its roots in animal life but to
all intelligence which flees the disconcerting complexity of
concrete realities, is that it creates for itself a world
of abstractions conforming to its reason or to the logic
of its desires. Gourmont believed that the intelligence,
an excellent instrument for making a priori constructions,
is especially inept at perceiving realities, and it is to this
infirmity that he attributes the numerous metaphysics,
religions, and moralities of the world. The role of the
intelligence is to comprehend and to classify, to relate a
phenomenon or a group of phenomena to an always
larger group. But perception of phenomena is the province
of the sensibility. Seen by the sensibility, the world is a
forest of differences. Each object retains its individual
quality and can be classified only by the perceiver's making
an abstraction of those differences. Abstraction therefore
is the province of the scientists, whose concern is quantity, not quality.

Abstract ideas tend to move away from "sensation" and
toward "sentiment." Gourmont's method of "dissociation
of ideas" is a means of leading those ideas back to the
sensations whence they took their origin, to the sensible
and empirically ascertainable reality. "Truth" can be seen
only through sensibility, but truth, Gourmont observed,
consists of "words." Therefore he proceeded to study
words—not the "rare" words of his symbolist period but

the development and evolution of meanings, those "crystallizations" of associations which words have acquired through the centuries. In this way he could get at the root of beliefs and prejudices: How did certain words acquire their particular meaning and how did they become emblems of "immutable truth?" This interest in philology led Gourmont to study the history of ideas—to show that in the world of ideas as well as in language, associations of ideas become consecrated by time and erected into verities, just as associations of words become clichés. His method was set forth in one of his most widely acclaimed articles, "La Dissociation des Idées" (1899), and exemplified in "Stéphane Mallarmé et l'Idée de Décadence" (1898), "La Gloire et l'Idée d'Immortalité" (1900), and "Le Succès et l'Idée de Beauté" (1901).[57] He described his method as follows:

> There are two ways of thinking. You can either accept current ideas and associations of ideas, just as they are, or else undertake, on your own account, new associations or, what is rarer, original dissociations. An intelligence capable of such efforts is, more or less, according to the degree, or according to the abundance and variety of its other gifts, a creative intelligence. It is a question either of inventing new relations between old ideas, old images, or of separating old ideas, old images united by tradition, of considering them one by one, being free to re-work them and arrange an infinite number of new couples which a fresh operation will disunite once more, and until new ties, always fragile and equivocal, are formed.[58]

"Truth," as it exists in the minds of most men, is composed of two elements, a fact and an abstraction, which gradually become, in the course of years of usage, an unassailable proposition. It becomes transformed and deformed, and finally, with the aid of tradition, becomes a commonplace. This process is the result of man's real need to possess some notions he can call "truths." Each corresponds to some "utility" and, when no longer useful, must be destroyed. "Most truths which travel the world (truths are great travelers) may be regarded as commonplaces, that is to say, associations of ideas common to a large number of men, none of whom would dare deliberately to dissociate them."

Gourmont explained that man, despite his propensity for lying, has a great respect for what he calls the "truth." It is his walking staff on his voyage through life; commonplaces are his daily bread and wine. Deprived of the truth of commonplaces, men find themselves defenseless, without support or nourishment. "They have such a great need for verities that they adopt new verities without rejecting the old; the brain of civilized man is a museum of contradictory verities." [59]

This causes no trouble, however, as man's mind is "successive." "He ruminates his truths one after another. He thinks as he eats." Certain analytical minds have tried to carry out an objective inventory of their own contradictions, but they have discovered that for each criticism raised by the reason, the emotions pose an impressive counter-argument; for as Gourmont said, citing the psychologist Ribot, "feelings are what are strongest in us in whom they represent permanence and continuity." An inventory of the contradictions of others is no less difficult, especially if it is a question of some one man in particular. One is confronted by hypocrisy, whose very social role it is to veil or to tone down "the excessive vividness of multi-colored convictions." It is therefore necessary to interrogate all men or at least large groups of them, in order that "the cynicism of some will compensate for the hypocrisy of others." The procedure is as follows: "It would perhaps be useful first to discover how ideas become associated and to what end. The manual of this operation is most simple; its principle is the analogy. . . . A great number of commonplaces have a historical origin: two ideas were united one day under the influence of events and that union was more or less durable."

For example, Europe, having seen with its own eyes the decline and death of Byzantium, coupled the two ideas, Byzantium-Decadence. This combination has be-

come a commonplace, an incontestable verity for all
literate persons and necessarily for all other people, who
cannot check on the verities handed down to them. The
critical mind, however, can consider a "truth" to represent
a commonplace as yet not dissociated and proceed to
trace it back to its origins, to take it apart and display
its component elements, much in the manner of a success-
ful chemical analysis. Then, with the débris of the former
"truth," one can construct a new truth more suitable to
current needs, which may be the exact opposite of its
predecessor. For man associates ideas not according to
logic or verifiable exactitude, but according to his pleasure and interests. Thus it is that most of his truths are
only prejudices or, at best, opinions.[60]

Gourmont found a curious example of these principles
in his examination of the present state of sexual morality.
This morality, peculiar to Christian peoples, is based on
the close association of two ideas, carnal pleasure and procreation. He traced the evolution, the alternate association
and dissociation of these ideas, from the ancient Egyptians
through the Greeks and the Christian Middle Ages to the
present day. Also, he saw a parallel conception in the
linkage of the ideas of physical pleasure and love. This
combination, sundered by medieval Christianity, had been
re-established by contemporary society. Nineteenth-century moralists were busily trying to combat the dissociation of love and procreation, and Gourmont was concerned lest they succeed.

In "Stéphane Mallarmé et l'Idée de Décadence" (*Culture des Idées*), Gourmont examined the notion of "decadence," which had come into vogue during the 1880's,
and analyzed the relation between it and other ideas with
which it had been associated at various times in its history.
He found that it had been coupled with the process of
physical death, as it occurs to the primitive mind, and with
the idea of punishment, as it occurs to the religious mind,
e.g., the decay of empires as the result of Jehovah's dis-
approval. But his main concern was with those misguided
historians who "naïvely" link a demonstrable political and

social decadence with literary decadence, and he rejected the popular notion that late Roman or late nineteenth-century literature was decadent at all. Such a misconception resulted from the academic tendency to deplore the decline of the familiar and traditional and to see the healthy desire for originality as a corruption of time-tested excellence. Gourmont pointed to the European eighteenth century as the prime example of true literary decadence and maintained that the idea of decadence should be associated with, if anything, the idea of imitation. Indeed, the "spirit of imitation" was, for Gourmont, the cause of the lifelessness of eighteenth-century poetry (a concept which, as Gourmont admitted, is itself subject to being dissociated).[61]

Gourmont's discussion of the history of the idea of decadence serves to introduce his defense of Mallarmé and the Symbolists in general, who were under fire by many popular critics of the Max Nordau school. In most of those attacks, Gourmont pointed out, the idea of decadence was being assimilated to its exact opposite—the idea of innovation. "But how have we come to regard as a peril every real innovation in art or in literature? Why, above all, is this assimilation one of the maladies peculiar to our time—perhaps the gravest of all, since it tends to restrict movement and to obstruct life?" Genius results in originality, and original creations, Gourmont asserts, are apt to appear obscure and excessively difficult to the majority of men. Therefore, unenlightened critics confused the difficulty of Mallarmé's poetry with what was actually supreme intelligence and originality, and so, in despair, pronounced it "decadent." In sum, most critics, in using the term decadence, construe its meaning exactly backwards. They attribute it to what is in actuality the most vital and healthy of modern literary endeavors: the Symbolists' striving for a closer union of sensibility and intellect, and their search for new language and new forms through which to express original insights.

Gourmont wrote several lengthy essays in dissociation, bearing such provocative titles as "Glory and the Idea of

Immortality" and "Success and the Idea of Beauty," and
he suggested many other traditional commonplaces deserving dissociative analysis: virtue-reward, vice-punish-
ment, crime-remorse, duty-happiness, God-goodness, au-
thority-respect, future-progress, unhappiness-punishment,
military-honor, beauty-sex, art-beauty, and "thousands of
others, some of which, although absurd, are useful to mankind."

In his intellectual exercises of dissociation, Gourmont
was obviously not concerned with pragmatic applications.
The "pure cult of ideas" has responsibilities only to the
perfection of its craft, and the fact that the world of practical life could not abide by the rules of such a craft
need not concern the specialist in free inquiry. As Kenneth Burke says, speaking of Gourmont, logical conclusions are not the concern of "a fine and free intelligence"
which dissociates ideas for love of the art and admits
"whatever intellectual exercise limbers the mind and fits
it for its proper state of 'disdainful nobility' (*dédaigneuse
noblesse*). His own method of dissociation provided him
with a striking stylistic device, a kind of mild schizo-
phrenia, whereby he could talk of dire things blithely.
And so he carried the logic of specialization to its ultimate conclusion, in acknowledging only a responsibility
to the principles of his profession." [62]

Two observations can be made here. First, it is true
that Gourmont, like Nietzsche, saw that ideas can operate
on two levels: a level of pure ideas having no practical
consequences, and a level of pragmatic ideas judged and
valued by their function in the world of practical affairs.
The second observation is that Gourmont's method, if
not always his practice, *can* have a function in the world of
practical life. In an era such as ours, dominated by political
and advertising propaganda consisting largely of reiterated
and dubious associations (Europe-decadence, Yankee-
imperialism, bigness-superiority, intellectuality-impracti-
cality, democracy-mediocrity, etc.), one might well engage in public and printed dissociations, not just for the
love of the art but for the clearer vision that might come
of such ideological manipulations.

Gourmont's method of dissociation of ideas was not entirely new; it was in the air of the times. His work is similar to the psychologist Théodule Ribot's treatise on the feelings, and has many affinities with the beliefs of the school of "psychologues" associated with the *Revue philosophique*. Also, Jules Renard, in his *Journal inédit* (1890), anticipated Gourmont: "One must operate by the dissociation and not by the association of ideas. An association is almost always banal. Dissociation disengages and reveals latent affinities."

But Gourmont brought this method to the attention of many American writers. Some, like Burke, welcomed dissociation as a valuable contribution to modern thought, and others, like Joseph Wood Krutch, viewed it mixed feelings, accusing Gourmont of being a strictly nihilistic exponent of nineteenth-century "scientific rationalism." [63] Krutch explained that the watchword of his own time (1928) had become "synthesis"—the opposite of the "analysis" which Gourmont advocated—construction instead of destruction. Such criticism seems to ignore Gourmont's intentions and his insistence that new structures must indeed be built—only not according to convention and habit, but according to the needs of man's true nature. Old associations must be destroyed only in order that new ones, more closely corresponding to contemporary needs, may be constructed and utilized as long as they serve man's interests. Studies in dissociation, though devoted to the annihilation of established ideas, were not entirely negative because, as Gourmont pointed out, new ideas and new truths can be formed from the rubble. Furthermore, as Burke says, the great emphasis which this method places upon *division* really serves to sharpen our understanding of *identification*. Also, contrary to Krutch's assertion that Gourmont's method is largely negative and of interest only to Gourmont's own generation, we must agree with Burke's opinion, given in 1950, that Gourmont rendered a positive service in showing that the factual side of "truths" often has no logical connection with the abstract, ideal side. "We need not accept the doctrine wholly as stated in his essay. We need not try to persuade ourselves that dissociation is the ultimate in intellectual prowess, since that very argument for dissociation is an association. But we can make out a strong case for it as a method for helping the initiate experimentally to break free of all topical assumptions, and thereby to cease being the victim of his own naïve rhetoric." [64]

It is regrettable that Gourmont did not carry his dissociation method further into the realm of literary criticism. His method was a development complementary to symbolism, which sought its effects precisely by utilizing the clusters of associations surrounding the important words of a poem or story. And, as Burke says, "any technical criticism of our methodological authors of today must concern itself with the further development and schematization of such ideas as de Gourmont was considering." [65]

Gourmont would doubtless have conceded that his method should be applied to the language of the poets as well as to the commonplaces of mankind in general. Words, he said, are signs, but they are also ciphers, and ciphers invite deciphering. But he also said that it is difficult to understand even the most sincere writing—and the author himself may fail to do so—because the meanings of words vary not only from one man to another but from one moment to another in the same time. "Language is thus a great cause of deception. It evolves in abstraction, and life evolves in the most concrete reality. Between the sentence and the things that the sentence designates, there is the distance between a landscape and a description of the landscape." [66]

This problem of the relationship of language and "reality," of abstraction and concreteness in language, will be discussed more fully in a later chapter on Gourmont's literary criticism, but for the moment we can observe that although Gourmont did not apply his method to the language of specific works of art, he advocated that others do so. However, he himself preferred to remain on the level of ideas and literature in general. In his essay in dissociation, "Stéphane Mallarmé et l'Idée de Déca-

dence," Gourmont analyzed the relationship of historical decadence and literary decadence, attacked the
linking of the ideas of innovation and experimentation
with the ideas of literary decadence, and posed his own
interpretation of decadence, associating it not with innovation, but with the eighteenth-century practice of spirit-
less imitation. He did not bring his method to bear upon
the language of Mallarmé's poetry as such; he remained in
the realm of the history of ideas, his objective being freedom of expression in the realm of creative writing in
general. Nevertheless, in defending Mallarmé and the
Symbolist writers against the attacks of the Max Nordau
school of literary moralists, he established, for other critics,
a philosophical and linguistic basis for a dissociative "explication de texte."

Gourmont was the "pure intellectual" in the way that
he loved, savored, and played with ideas as being more
real than life itself—"intelligence for intelligence's sake."
Thought became an intellectual game or a supremely disinterested exercise; superior detachment became the essence of the intelligent mind. He never recoiled before the
free play of intellect; he fearlessly and sometimes out-
rageously carried it to its logical extremes. He desired
only to present "the succession of his mental postures at
different moments of his existence in the face of different
problems." [67] But he made it clear with an ironic smile
that games of pure intellect are played in a world that is
not to be identified too closely with the practical world
wherein the element of intellect scarcely enters. One must
not oppose the practical world heedlessly, for it is not
always wise to flout social custom. "If incredulity counsels
absolute immorality, the mature and non-believing mind
very quickly discovers that relative immorality alone is
compatible with the social condition." It is possible, however, to maintain a "free mind" in the domain of thought
by following this formula: "Treat all subjects as if you
were meeting them for the first time; accept no ready-
made opinion; be one who instructs himself in proportion
as he observes; dissociate ideas and acts; do not be the

dupe of any philosophical construct; reduce it immediately to its component parts; have no belief."

In short, one should feel at all times disengaged from all ties and capable of making new departures. To be free is above all to disengage one's own personality, to create for oneself an individual law conforming with one's own nature and to realize oneself according to that law, "in proportion to one's forces and the obstacles opposed by society."

But to conquer oneself is a heroic act. To maintain an original personality against a milieu that wants to remodel its members and gather them all into "the average type" takes great rebellious energy. Hence Gourmont, lacking Christian faith, could admire many of the saints, especially a Saint Paul or a Saint Francis of Assisi, who were in their own way free and proud spirits, determined to create for themselves a unique destiny and to separate themselves from the herd.

Gourmont's ideal of intellectual honesty frequently resulted, as we have already noted, in self-contradiction. As one of his critics expressed it, his works became "a display of contrary affirmations." Gourmont concealed nothing; therefore, whenever he formulated an affirmation, he knew that he would someday encounter the opposite position, view it as also presenting claims to legitimacy, and he would be obliged to treat it with equal consideration. Indeed, Gourmont accepted and seemed to enjoy his contradictions—as a *divertissement* of rare quality, a *jeu d'esprit* of a very aristocratic nature. But there is something to Brunet's complaint that Gourmont lent himself too voluptuously to his contradictions instead of taking them as themes for meditation. To accept oneself in a fundamental contradiction is admirable boldness, but it may also be an unconscious way of dodging a problem. As Brunet said, "After all, it is at the collision point of our contradictions that our most profound and decisive problems are posed." Which is why, even in Gourmont's lucid and penetrating mind, problems of the first order often remain in a blurred and unresolved state—for example, the problem of the relationship of liberty and order, and of originality and tradition. Gourmont's skepticism does in fact reveal a certain confusion and softness, as some of his critics—Brunet, Gide, Léautaud—insist. Sometimes he was too flexible, as if all opinions were equal and had the same reasons for existing. Although many points of view are possible and legitimate, they do not all have the same quality, and the values of the relationships which they express are not identical.

Gourmont was accused by one critic, oddly enough, of not being a skeptic at all. Paul Léautaud, who often visited Gourmont in the offices of the *Mercure de France*, stated that his friend's great disdain, skepticism, and aristocratic detachment was just a "mask." This is a reference to Gourmont's later years, when he had become amorously involved with the "Amazone," a situation revealing an emotional and at times almost sentimental Gourmont. But a more important point was raised by Léautaud when he stressed, by way of "proof" that Gourmont was not fundamentally skeptical, Gourmont's embracing of science and finding in it almost a new "religion." Gourmont's attitude reflected the "naïve zeal" of the neophyte in throes of discovery and revelation. He did not have his usual doubts, said Léautaud, regarding the words and beliefs of "savants"; he accepted and "believed" them and treated the doubters as "impious." [68]

The criticisms do not do justice to Gourmont. What Gourmont embraced so fervently was not the words and beliefs of scientists so much as their *method* of ascertaining truth. It was the scientific method that appealed to him—its empiricism, its tentativeness, and its experimental attitude toward human problems. He had no use for either the dogma of religion or the dogma of certain positivists who "misread" the message of science. Gourmont liked the "laws" of science because, strictly speaking, they are not laws at all but working hypotheses, provisional descriptions of phenomena, always subject to revision in the light of new evidence. Like Gourmont's own method, the scientific method was analytical, skeptical in the sense of taking nothing for granted, and flexible in its receptivity to new or contradictory theory. Most important, it relied strictly upon the evidence of the senses, which, for all their fallibility, are our sole means of apprehending fact. Nobody could be harder than Gourmont on those disciples of science who accepted its findings as immutable or absolute. He never believed for a minute that it would solve all of man's problems or even bring him happiness, but as far as ascertaining relative truth is concerned, he found it to be the best and in fact the only method we have. Gourmont was quick to censure the scientist who, wandering outside the realm of scientific method, made lofty and dogmatic pronouncements of a theological nature. An Eddington in the 1940's would have fared as poorly at Gourmont's hands as Berthelot did in his time.

Nevertheless, there was often a marked disparity between the theory and the practice of Gourmont's skepticism. As Marc Denkinger points out, Gourmont's life was a perpetual battle in favor of aesthetic, moral, and scientific principles, and far from fleeing "the horrible mania for certitude," he many times seemed to be seeking it.[69] In his later years he was fond of speaking in terms of "laws," as when he made over Quinton's law of thermal constancy in the evolution of vertebrates into his own "Loi de la Constance intellectuelle" in the evolution of the human species. Similarly, in his *Physique de l'Amour* he spoke quite dogmatically on the subject of the "laws of nature" that govern sexuality, and in his earlier days he took a very unskeptical attitude toward his own rigid principles in the realm of literary values.

Gourmont freely admitted that man must have "truths" to live by, but that each person should fashion his own truths in response to the needs of his own sensibility and temperament. He should refuse to accept the ready-made truths of the populace, those founded on prejudice, hearsay, or habit. Personal truths should be adopted only after a painstaking examination, a "dissociation," and be based on the best available scientific evidence. Furthermore, they must be subject to change or modification, or for that matter, outright contradiction. (Gourmont's revisions of his theories on subjective idealism would serve as an example—and he insisted that his opinions were always subject to his own process of dissociation.) The pursuit of personal truth must work through destruction and negation. The old and established truths must be razed, and out of the rubble each man must build anew according to the needs of his own being, for it is only by truths thus discovered that man can live in harmony with himself and nature.

3   GOURMONT'S
LITERARY CRITICISM

GOURMONT, as one of the editors of the *Mercure de France*, wrote very little literary criticism during the first half of the 1890's. He and his colleagues were too much involved in polemics, attacks, and defenses to reflect upon the formulation of critical principles. Around 1896, however, the situation had altered. The period of battles was nearly over and the days of manifestoes were past; it was time for editors to produce anthologies of the new poetry and for Gourmont to consider writing the *Livres des Masques*. From then on, there was a tendency to look upon Symbolism retrospectively. A calmer atmosphere, favorable to criticism, replaced the atmosphere of credos, challenges, and rebuttals. Now, in the usually embattled pages of the *Mercure de France*, there appeared general reflections on criticism. Formerly, the emphasis had been on precepts of creation; now the *Mercure* emphasized evaluation of results by means of critical analysis and contested in more philosophical terms the enemies of Symbolism and subjectivism in art.[1]

Beginning in 1896 Gourmont became indirectly involved in an interesting debate on critical principles. Charles Maurras, in his "Essai sur la Critique," [2] had advanced several precepts in support of the subjective approach to literature and proclaimed that the critic is as much a creator as the poet. In his mode of creation, he said, the critic knows but one rule—"the consent of the sensibility to the beauty evoked." The critic follows no

lead but that of his own pleasure. A few months later
Robert de Souza replied to Maurras and countered with a
eulogy of traditional criticism. The critic does not create,
Souza maintained. On the contrary, "he must decompose
the essence" of the work, that is, "recognize it and disengage it." [3]

Gourmont did not take direct part in this debate, but
his views were reflected in the preface to his second
Livre des Masques. He sided with Maurras, but he did so
by relating his new attitudes to his earlier principles. In
1892 he had appealed to the intellect of his readers; now
he recognized the "arbitrage" of sensation and insisted
that there is no common measure between two writers:

> We no longer have principles, and there are no longer
> models; a writer creates his esthetic in creating his work;
> we have reached the point where we must call on sensation
> more often than judgment. In literature, as in everything,
> the reign of abstract words must end. A work of art exists
> only through the emotion it gives us; it is sufficient to
> determine and characterize the nature of that emotion;
> that will take us from metaphysics to sensuality, from the
> pure idea to physical pleasure.[4]

These precepts, which are the formulation of Gourmont's theory of Impressionistic criticism, were fore-
shadowed in an earlier essay, written in 1893, entitled
"L'Art libre et l'Esthètique individuelle." [5] Although
written at the height of his Symbolist period, this essay
was one of Gourmont's first attempts to draw upon natural science to support aesthetic theory. Devoted to the
belief that "Art is anterior to Esthetics, and therefore
Esthetics must be an explication and not a theory of Art,"
Gourmont drew analogies from Perrier's *Colonies ani-
males* to establish the relativity of aesthetic judgment.
He wanted to prove that the individual is "anormal" and
"a being dissimilar from those beings which resemble
him the most." On the authority of Perrier, Gourmont
stated that, in the scale of life, members of a group of
creatures are increasingly dissimilar in proportion as they

are more perfected; that is, the higher animals show far greater variety among themselves than do the lower. Therefore, if superior beings differ among themselves radically, their aesthetic production, being a personal creation, will differ no less radically. Consequently, there can be no common measure between two works of art, no possible "judgment of comparison," no aesthetic which, applicable to one work of art, is applicable to another; no pre-fabricated rules. Gourmont quoted Kant in support of this contention: "The principle of judgment of taste which we call esthetic can only be subjective"; and he concluded that one can judge only as one creates, "according to individual and personal rules"—by impressionist criticism.

This early statement had to be modified later, especially the idea that there is "no possible judgment of comparison" between works, if Gourmont were to function at all intelligibly as a critic; for, as he said later, the business of the critic is "analysis and comparison." But he held to his conviction that standards of judgment and comparison are in the last analysis highly personal, the product of the individual sensibility. In the essay, "Le Succès et l'Idée de Beauté," [6] Gourmont made it clear that all aesthetic judgment is referable to one basic criterion: pleasure. He repeated that there is no arbiter other than the sensibility for appreciating the beauty of a work. However, he distinguished between two types of sensibility: he opposed the sensibility of the "vulgar" to that of persons "capable of an original esthetic emotion." In other words, he created what he called an "esthetic caste." Beauty for most people is derived from the "sexual origins of art"; it is, as Stendhal said, based on "the promise of happiness." The aesthetic judgment of the vulgar is "the naive avowal of pleasure" and is dependent on the extent to which the person can relate the art work to the experiences of his own life. The sensibility of the "esthetic caste" may be as spontaneous as that of the common folk, but it is a more complicated affair. It is "a mixture of beliefs, traditions, calculations, habits, conceptions: it involves respect, fear, and an obscure appetite for novelty." Yet its aesthetic experience is more apt to derive from the art-object itself than from its associative emotions.

An important aspect of this new attitude toward the problem of literary judgment is that Gourmont no longer appealed to the intellect capable of objective evaluation, but rather to the extremely complicated sensibility capable of an emotion at once very complex in origin and "pure" in quality—that is, purely aesthetic.[7] Furthermore, in his conclusion to "Le Succès et l'Idée de Beauté," Gourmont showed how his new emotionalist criteria, judgment based on sensation, are sure to be more responsible than the more traditional aesthetics: "The sensibility is incorruptible, the popular sensibility as well as that of the literary coterie: it is as incorruptible as taste and smell . . . Let men freely seek their pleasures. . . . What is beautiful is what moves us; but we cannot be moved except in proportion to our emotional receptivity and according to the state of our nervous system."

Gourmont recognized that this was his own approach to literature—judgment corresponding to an excitation of the sensibility, but he realized his obligation to found personal preferences and pleasures on a more general principle. "Erecting into laws one's personal impressions" might be the duty of the sincere critic, but it does not ensure that his findings will have any significance for others. Therefore, Gourmont was careful to explain that the critic who formulates the tastes and interests of his caste is "determined" by his education and heredity and is therefore involuntarily the guardian of a tradition, and that the more he consults his sensibility, the more he will be faithful to that role. Gourmont believed that the sensibility of the aesthetic caste, which the critic represents, demands novelty and originality, but this does not mean that its judgments are as faddish or transitory as those of the masses. Tradition is built into the superior sensibility. The task of the critic, therefore, is to set this tradition, this sense of beauty and value crystallized through the centuries, against the facile enthusiasms of the crowd. Thus Gourmont, in modifying his earlier emphasis on the importance of novelty in art, established the universality of impressionist criticism. His earlier concern for novelty resulted from his determination to ensure a place for Symbolism in the French literary hierarchy, but the more those days of struggle receded into the background, the more Gourmont became concerned with "tradition" and Symbolism's relation to it.

Gourmont recognized that for himself literary criticism was primarily an artistic exercise, "the transposition of an emotion into signs." But on the other hand, he affirmed that all superior sensibility is in perfect harmony with the general sensibility of its caste and its period, which in turn is composed, in large part, of hereditary attitudes and "superstitions." Thus, in Gourmont's opinion the critic who judges in accordance with his sensibility performs the feat of uniting the present and the past into the same emotion. He is well prepared to show his own generation, usually avid for novelties, the beauties of the past, and he is also equipped to relegate contemporary art to its proper place in scale of values in terms of historical perspective. Judging the aesthetic quality of a work by virtue of superior sensibilities is the act of establishing, consciously or half consciously, a *rapprochement* between the work, our current literary "ideal," and the ideal of the past. This function of criticism, therefore, justifies Gourmont's sensualist method.

Gourmont began by being highly critical of the theories of Taine and Sainte-Beuve, especially of their stress on biographical and environmental influences at the expense of the intrinsic value of the work of art. But he ended by reflecting rather obviously much of Taine's thought and by finding reasons to praise the criticism of Sainte-Beuve. Gourmont's belief in the generalized sensibility of the aesthetic caste had much in common, for example, with Taine's "personnage regnant" and Sainte-Beuve's "famille d'esprits." [8] Furthermore, the superior sensibility, as Gourmont conceived it, is determined by cultural and hereditary conditions strongly suggesting

Taine's "race, moment, and milieu." Gourmont came to terms completely with his precursor in his essay on "Sainte-Beuve, Créateur de Valeurs" (1904).[9] He found the great Romantic critic to be, in fact, an impressionist critic, one who does not judge by intellect alone. Despite the scientific approach and the explanation of a work by biography and milieu, Sainte-Beuve's criticisms were valid because "good literary judgments are not purely intellectual: they include considerable feeling." He judged by "his sympathetic faculties."

In this essay Gourmont re-states his belief that only the sensibility in harmony with its entire generation is capable of "re-making" literature in the image of its own society and period. The critic's function is to re-make past literature for his own time; he must renew "motives for admiration" and present a work under new aspects. Many a legend or popular tale, Gourmont reminds us, never acquired its proper value, even though many persons knew it by heart, because that legend or tale never found a critic to extract its value. Sainte-Beuve, of all the critics of his time, was best able to establish the value of a work. He especially had "the power to fix durably the image of one of his contemporaries or to lead opinion to revise its former judgments. . . . The critic who is a creator of values is even more rare than the great poet." [10]

Sainte-Beuve was the great critic of Romanticism, and, according to Gourmont, France owes its understanding of that movement to Sainte-Beuve's re-creation of it, especially his establishing the contribution of Chateaubriand. Similarly, current views of Ronsard and the Pléiade, and of Port-Royal, derive from that same critic, the creator of values:

> His method, or rather the method, for there is only one, is the renewing of motives. Bossuet has been constantly admired for three centuries: but in each century the motives, or grounds, for admiration have changed. What changes them is creative criticism. In renewing the premises of our judgment, he renews the judgment itself, though not necessarily fundamentally; and the work, under

that unexpected illumination, appears fresh and almost new.[11]

In sum, the judgments of Sainte-Beuve "created the literary values according to which we judge in our turn." And this is what Gourmont tried to do in his own work, even before he had formulated this view of Sainte-Beuve. His own *Le Latin mystique* (1892) was an effort at "le renouvellement des motifs" of an old literature.

To many readers of modern literature the name of Remy de Gourmont is synonymous with "impressionist" criticism. He has been grouped with other "personal" writers such as Anatole France and Jules Lemaître, to whom criticism was the recounting, in France's well-known words, of "the adventures of a soul among masterpieces." This phrase, and all that it suggests in the way of irresponsible subjectivism, might describe some of Gourmont's critical activity, but surely does not apply to his best work; for Gourmont's criticism, after a period of vacillation, ultimately synthesized traditional scholarly criticism and an original sensualist impressionism. He began as a more or less conventional scholar of ideas and ended by developing a method of literary evaluation that not only differed from the method of those very impressionists with whom his name has been linked, but often was sharply critical of them.

Impressionism was already a well-known mode of criticism when Gourmont joined the fray in the early 1890's, and it had been attacked by influential scholars, notably Brunetière. A writer of formidable erudition and thoroughness, Brunetière had stressed what he believed to be the "menace" to scholarly study inherent in a subjective approach to literature, and so it was Brunetière who received the full force of Gourmont's counterattack. But the critical differences between the two men should not obscure fundamental similarities. Gourmont was a match for Brunetière in depth and scope of learning but was reluctant, except in a few cases like *Le Latin mystique*, to risk losing what he felt to be the vital elements of criticism—the insights of sensibility and intelligence—by submerging them in a mass of scholarly apparatus. Also, both men enlisted the aid of contemporary thought and sought to base their aesthetic doctrines on the findings of natural science. But each asked different questions and received different answers. Brunetière wanted authority, control, scientific classifications, impersonality in criticism, and morality in art. Gourmont wanted individualism, freedom from classification, justification of personality in criticism, and rejection of moral criteria in matters of art. Brunetière's theories brought him to view contemporary literature, by and large, with hostility and contempt, whereas Gourmont's theories brought him to a spirited defense of modern experimental writing.

Brunetière's views were set forth clearly in his "La critique impressioniste" (January 1891).[12] In this essay he focused his attack on the subjectivism of Anatole France, Jules Lemaître, and Paul Desjardins. He deplored their insistence on man's inability to "get out of himself" and maintained that objective criticism is not only possible but is the only valid criticism. The critic must fix the exact date, the moment of literary history, the social surroundings, the circumstances amid which the author worked, his personality and character. He can then try, after such explanations, to classify and judge the work. This is the whole object of criticism, Brunetière claimed: "What do we see there that is not *objective*, that is not or cannot be independent of the personal tastes and private sympathies of the critic who tries to explain, classify, and judge?" And, in support of his insistence on the "classification of genres," he cited, as Gourmont was fond of doing on his own behalf, various scientists who favored the principle of classification: Haeckel, Agassiz, Mill, Comte, Darwin, and T. H. Huxley.

Furthermore, said Brunetière, if a work of art were merely the expression of the individuality of the artist, not only criticism but art itself would perish. Like T. S. Eliot after him, Brunetière saw at the basis of impressionist criticism the would-be creative artist. He cited the efforts at original composition by Lemaître, Desjardins, and France, and stated that criticism was *not* their main ambition. He saw an important distinction between the artist and the critic: What makes the originality of the artist *is* his impressionist, subjective, and truly personal way of seeing and feeling. The artist "adds to his art the individuality of his own sensations." But merits in a poet or novelist become faults in a critic. The fashion of intervening in person may greatly assist the novelty of impressions, but does it not affect justice and truth? He grants that France, Lemaître, and Desjardins are occasionally correct in their judgments because of their superior stature—their intelligence and erudition. But, he asked, what of their lesser and more ignorant followers? They would be a threat to the relationship between literature and history. It is the business of criticism, Brunetière concluded, to think and judge for the people who are too occupied or unable to analyze and perceive quality. Criticism must teach them to judge, to discriminate, to compare, and to classify; and these vital functions impressionist criticism failed to perform.

This, then, is the kind of heavy attack impressionism was under during the 'nineties, and Gourmont faced his enemy squarely in the essay, "M. Brunetière" (*Prom. litt.* III). While not defending Lemaître, France, and Desjardins themselves—for he had his own reservations about the quality of their work—he did analyze the implications of Brunetière's theories and pose his own counter-aesthetic.

Gourmont stated flatly, in his opening sentence, that he did not believe in the conventional "hierarchical distinctions" between critics and creators. He refused to admit, for example, that Taine might be less creative than his "contemporary in time," Octave Feuillet, or that Aristotle might be less creative than his "contemporary in space," Shakespeare. Whether one writes a novel or a history of French literature, "it is a question, if one is to construct a work, of establishing new relationships between known facts. . . . it is a matter of providing new grounds for understanding or new grounds for feeling: in both cases there is creation." The two types of writer work in different ways, but they have in common the obligation to be original or to be nothing at all. Both must be "creators of values," one in the order of the sensibility, the other in the order of the intelligence, and, as we have seen, intelligence is only an aspect of sensibility. In sum, "as much genius is needed for one to be a great critic as to be a great novelist."

Gourmont hastened to add that he did not mean to say that Brunetière was a genius, but he admitted that he could not see how Brunetière could be considered inferior to or less creative than his contemporary, Paul Bourget, and he suspected that the critic's work would outlive the novelist's. "The critic is needed for coordination and, even more, for architecture. He may not shape the stones, but he gives them the place which is suitable in the ensemble of the monument." At one time in his career Brunetière realized this rather well, Gourmont pointed out, but he chose to graft his critical method on to Darwinism. Why? Because Darwin, like other historians of animal life, made abstractions of individuals. Natural history knows only species, and it implies, as a rule, that all normal individuals of one species, at any one given moment, are identical. Gourmont insisted that this scientific method pleased Brunetière because it permitted him to combat individualism, which had always appeared to him both a social and an intellectual menace. To be sure, it is necessary, if a critic is to speak of personal creations, to mention persons; but, Gourmont replied, authors always took second rank in Brunetière's works. In Brunetière's hands, literary history was no longer a succession of portraits of individual lives; rather it was Poetry or History that was studied, and not poets or historians. In using Brunetière's method, one would examine works without giving much importance to the authors, and one would show how works engender one another by "natural necessity"; how the "species poetry" gives birth to the "varieties sonnet and madrigal"; how, under the influence of milieu, the "variety lyricism" is transformed, without losing its essential character, into "eloquence"; and many other such metamorphoses.

From this form of "madness," Gourmont assures us, Brunetière soon recovered, only to react violently against the position he had just abandoned. From his unfruitful contact with science, Brunetière retained only a painful memory. Having been unable to bend science to his own predetermined use, he believed it was not good for anything. When science had not responded satisfactorily to his interrogations about the evolution of literary genres, he believed that it was incapable of *any* useful responses, and he impetuously proclaimed it to be a failure. This was Brunetière's second "madness" and the one which achieved "his reputation as the most reasonable of all men." The basic problem, Gourmont points out, was a religious one. Brunetière, among others, hoped that science would bring certainty into the realm of religion, metaphysics, and morality; but science brought only negations, and more negations—proffered with a grand air of indifference. There followed a great disillusionment, and those who suffered from it tended to revert back to the "old traditional affirmations." The failure of science that Brunetière proclaimed was, in fact, a "metaphysical failure."

Brunetière, then, reverted not only to traditional faith but to traditional authority as well. He wished to restore the spirit of authority in all domains and to make men understand that there is governing them a "will to order," to which they must submit their instincts, their sensibilities, perhaps even their reason. He wished to teach that all activity must be regulated and limited by rules, in politics as in grammar, in morality as in art, for it is necessary that one accept that universal authority for oneself and, having accepted it, impose it on others. Brunetière had found all these principles in Catholicism, Gourmont believed, a Catholicism which he had actually never abandoned, as shown by his abiding taste for Bossuet and the seventeenth-century classicists and his hostility to most all modern literature.

For Gourmont, Brunetière's work was a valuable repertory of facts, ideas, and literary judgments, but nothing more. He had only "objective ideas, those which are the product of a will or a method which one acquires." Those ideas were often reasonable, even correct, but not original. Brunetière lacked the "ferment of idealism" when he insisted that "the same reality is imposed on all intelligences; and, of each thing, there is but one vision that is exact and 'in conformity with the object,' just as, for each fact, there is but one formula that is scientific."

To Gourmont's mind this quote, better than a lengthy discourse, showed the limits of Brunetière's intellect and critical position. Such principles bring the critic to deny the legitimacy of all individual activity. Originality becomes a breach of taste, and art disappears. Indeed, every object and every fact then admits of only *one* valid and true representation, and ideas are necessarily divided into two classes: the true and the untrue. Gourmont concluded that one must remain firmly with the "unassailable principle" of subjective idealism—"the world is my representation." It is "the only fecund principle, the only one which permits, which demands, the free development of intellects and sensibilities."

The critical theory which Gourmont was eventually to evolve, however, would not have entirely displeased Brunetière. Gourmont was to be commended by T. S. Eliot and others for his erudition, his sense of history and sense of fact, his insistence on sincerity, and his advocacy of analysis and comparison as the bases of a responsible criticism—in other words, attributes and principles favored by Brunetière. Furthermore, an impartial observer would probably grant, in evaluating the two critics' positions, that although Brunetière's methods were unduly doctrinaire and his judgments prejudiced and at times narrowly moral, his insistence on the necessity of studying the influence of works on other works and of seeking in periods of transition the seeds of the art to follow, was a necessary counter-balance to Gourmont's early tendency to overemphasize the possibility of independent and spontaneous generation in literature.

ii

Gourmont differed sharply and openly with those who questioned the principle of subjectivism in criticism, but he also differed openly, if less sharply, with some of the critics who embraced that principle. He rejected the assumptions on which Brunetière based his attack on Anatole France and Jules Lemaître, but he had some doubts of his own about the quality of those critics' judgments, and they in turn tended almost completely to ignore Gourmont's work.

During the 1880's and 1890's Jules Lemaître was writing his own "impressionistic" critiques of contemporary authors. Along with Anatole France he produced an important body of criticism founded on the principles that "one pronounces good what one loves, and that is all there is to it" and "I am sure of my impressions." [13] One would expect that such views would have placed Lemaître in close personal company with Gourmont, but in fact, despite a great mutual respect, they were not especially fraternal. For one thing, their differences on the subject of Symbolism were fundamental. As we have seen, both Lemaître and France were extremely hostile to the new movement, seeing in it a lack of human values, an absence of traditional clarity of expression, and violations of principles of good writing. In other respects, however, the views of the three critics were quite similar. Lemaître, for example, described the work of the critic in this rather obscure manner:

> One should first of all analyze the impression he receives of the book; then he should try to define the author, that is, to describe his "form" and his temperament, what the world is to him and what he seeks by preference, what is his feeling about life, what is the species and degree of his sensibility; finally, how his mind works. In brief, one should try to determine, according to the impression one receives of the author, the impression which he himself receives of things. [14]

This has much in common with Gourmont's own conception of the critic's role. His criticism represents the eternal pursuit of sensations and emotions in the writings of others, the attempt to recover and to re-live the initial sensation experienced by the writer before composition. After having sought and presumably found the initial feelings of an author, "the impression that he himself receives of things," Gourmont would proceed, in the manner described by Lemaître, to account for the experience in terms of the author's "temperament," the "degree and species of his sensibility," and his "preferences and sentiments about life." But for all his sensuality, Gourmont insisted upon sincerity. To be sure, in the preface to his *Divertissements* he dismissed sincerity as unnecessary to the writing of poetry—which perhaps accounts for the weakness of his own poetic efforts—but elsewhere, and in his literary criticism above all, he saw literary value in terms of honesty of feeling. Art is, or should be, based on concrete sensation, faithfully transcribed by the artist, just as good criticism is dependent upon the sincerity of the critic in explaining his own impressions.

This accounts for the "confessional" quality of Gourmont's work observed by many of his critics. In the preface to his *Livres des Masques*, Gourmont explained this confessional element by claiming it to be the only justification for writing. The only reason a man has for writing, he insisted, is to express himself; the only excuse is to be original. He must create his aesthetic for himself.[15] Seven years later, in 1903, Gourmont expanded this idea, asserting that one always writes of himself in criticism as well as in other genres: "Criticism is perhaps the most subjective of all the literary genres; it is a perpetual confession; while we believe that we are analyzing the works of others, it is ourselves that we are unveiling and exposing to the public." [16]

He believed that this necessity explains why criticism is usually so mediocre and so often fails to hold our attention, even when it deals with questions of vital interest to us: "In fact, in order to be a good critic, a man must have a strong personality; he must be able to impose himself and to rely not on the choice of subjects but on the value of his own mind. In art the subject matters little; at least it is never more than one of the parts of art; the subject is no more important in criticism: it is never anything but a pretext." [17]

This passage is significant, as Martin Turnell points out, because it draws attention to three important elements of criticism, usually lacking in the work of Taine and Sainte-Beuve. First, it insists on the personal factor in criticism—a corrective to the nineteenth-century attempt to reduce criticism to an exact science. Second, it shows not only that there is no substitute for personal sensibility but also that this alone is not enough—the force of personality and mind is equally important. Third and most important, in Turnell's estimation, we see "a distinguished critic asserting *for the first time* that criticism is valuable for its own sake and is not (as Taine tried to make it) a branch of some other science." Turnell adds a footnote to this statement: "As far as I am aware it is not until 1921 that we find an English critic making a similar declaration. In that year, Mr. Middleton Murry wrote in an article called 'A Critical Credo': 'The function of criticism is, therefore, primarily the function of literature itself, to provide a means of expression for the critic.' " [18] Turnell could have added that since Middleton Murry was one of the English critics most under the influence of Remy de Gourmont (his *Problem of Style* owed much to *Le Problème du Style*), it is not surprising that he should echo the French critic.

Gourmont justified his theories of criticism by stressing the reliability of judgment based on a sensibility which is shared by other members of one's generation. Jules Lemaître, on the other hand, defended his Impressionism by pointing out the changeability of all things, both subjective and objective. For this reason, Lemaître believed, literary criticism cannot have a doctrine: the only certainty is the impression of the moment. Tradition is artificial, and the only value of criticism, or of any other genre, is the representation of a personal world. Its destiny is to become merely the art of enjoying books: "Dogmatic at first, [criticism] has become historical and scientific, but it does not seem that its evolution has ended. Vain as doctrine, necessarily incomplete as science, it perhaps tends to become simply the art of enjoying books and through them enriching and improving one's impressions." [19]

Gourmont was in complete agreement with this anti-doctrinaire statement, as far as it goes. In an essay on Jules Lemaître he admitted that his criticism has "the merits of clarity, acuteness and good sense." Gourmont added, however, that "we may regret that it has not also, not principles which it can very well do without, but a direction. It indeed moves forward rather at random." Gourmont believed in the necessity of a "literary faith"; it is the "most fortunate of intellectual disciplines." He explained that thereby we learn "to judge by other motives than our personal taste"; we feel the "necessity for certain aesthetic sacrifices"; we learn that "even in a limited field works may have a social interest independent of their art interest." He summed up by stating that "the great defect of M. Jules Lemaître's criticism is that it had no object; it lacked force, because its author lacked discipline." [20]

This sounds rather strange coming from Gourmont. We are more accustomed to hearing paeans to the virtues of liberty, subjectivism, originality, and so forth. But this essay was written in 1903, by which time Gourmont had somewhat modified his literary anarchism. Furthermore, it is true that this anarchism had been developed and expounded on behalf of a definite movement, Symbolism, which provided the "discipline" that he claimed to be necessary. As he said in the same essay, "Apart from certain initiatory books [livres initiateurs], almost all literature derives its value from its conformity with a momentary aesthetic ideal . . . It was the misfortune of some of our contemporaries, who were highly gifted, that they were neither Parnassians nor Naturalists nor Symbolists."

Thus we see the protean Gourmont, defending complete freedom of expression when confronted by doctrinaire and traditionalist critics, and then demanding discipline and restraints on judgment by personal taste when confronted by a critic even more independent than himself. This should not be attributed to insincerity, however, for it is not entirely to Gourmont's discredit that he was capable of revising his own arguments and taking the opposite view to one previously held, if the weight of evidence seemed to have shifted. He was far more afraid of rigidity of mind than of inconsistency. He would have liked Henri Peyre's observation that "the ravage caused by systematic intellects in criticism lies before us. The worst errors of judgment have usually been caused by the critic's obstinate blinkers when he shut himself up in the dungeon of his preordained theory and lost his ability to enjoy new works which did not readily fall into his tyrannical rules or his neat pigeonholes." Peyre quotes Baudelaire to the effect that a system "is a kind of damnation which drives us to a perpetual abjuration; one must unceasingly invent a new one, and thus endure cruel punishment." [21] And Gourmont, however much he insisted that the critic should "remake his aesthetic" for each new work of art while still retaining adherence to a literary faith, never wavered from the central core of his theories: his conviction that the individually cultivated sensibility is the only reliable source of literary judgment.

iii

Gourmont's tendency to reverse positions has resulted in some difference of opinion among his critics as to the extent, if any, of his rejection of Symbolism toward the turn of the century. Albert Lippman, in his "Remy de Gourmont: the First Thirty Years," [22] maintains that Symbolism was only an episode in Gourmont's development and that it did not represent the "true" Gourmont. Lippman points out that Gourmont began with an interest in ideas and scholarship, rejected them for a time while experimenting with Symbolism, and then returned to his earlier and more fundamental interests.

Edmund Gosse believed that "Gourmont became tired of Symbolism rather suddenly, and buried it in two volumes which were the best he had yet published." The *Livres des Masques* of 1896 and 1898 marked, in Gosse's opinion, "the beginning of the author's permanent work as a critic of letters." Later in the essay he repeated that "at the close of the century Remy de Gourmont abandoned symbolism, and the world of ideas took possession of him." [23]

Garnet Rees, on the other hand, denies that any significant change took place in Gourmont's attitude. He maintains that the *Livres des Masques* were not an "autopsy" but rather an "ausculation" of Symbolism.[24] It is true that Gourmont was seeking a new form of expression, but this did not involve rejection of Symbolism. Gourmont's evolution, according to Rees, consisted of an extension of basic Symbolist principles.

The problem here, and the source of differences, would appear to lie in the confusion as to just what was meant by "basic Symbolist principles." If Gosse had in mind a certain literary technique rather than a general philosophy of literature, then his assertion would have to be accepted as true. Gourmont did in fact abandon his preciosity, his taste for the excessively bizarre, the decadent interest in rare words and feelings, and so on. But Symbolism did not mean just these things to him; in fact the emphasis lay quite elsewhere. As shown in earlier chapters, Symbolism was for Gourmont a general philosophy of literature, based on two principles: the idea of liberty and the cult of art. That these principles continued to be the basis of literary activity for Gourmont is demonstrated by three definitions he gave, revealing the essential flexibility of his conception of Symbolism. The first, which is most frequently cited as summing up Gourmont's aesthetic, appeared in the preface to his first *Livre des Masques*, written in 1896, and is worth quoting at length:

> What is meant by Symbolism? Almost nothing, if we keep to its narrow and etymological meaning; if we go beyond, it can mean individualism in literature, freedom

in art, abandonment of the formulas taught, tendencies towards what is new, strange and even bizarre; it may also mean idealism, disdain for the social anecdote, anti-Naturalism, the tendency to take from life only the characteristic detail, to pay attention only to the act by which one man is distinguished from another, to wish to achieve only results, the essential; finally, for poets symbolism seems bound to free verse, that is to say verse freed from its swaddling clothes, verse whose young body can disport at its ease, away from bonds and clothing.

Let us admit then that Symbolism is the expression, even if excessive, untimely, and pretentious, of individualism in art.

This definition was based on what Gourmont considered to be its most original aspect, "the principle of the ideality of the world," and it is general enough to permit its author considerable latitude. As he said in his second definition, written in January 1902, "There is a manner of being symbolist, as there is a manner of being romantic, which does not include—indeed to the contrary—the abandonment of the esthetic personality." This manner, moreover, obliges its practitioners to maintain "the disdain which from the beginning they showed for all literature without ideas and without taste, denuded of intellectuality or of a profound feeling of life and mystery." "To remain symbolist, after ten or fifteen years, is to refuse to participate in the universal indulgence; it is always to obey the ancient vow to maintain, against the vulgarizers, the nobility of art and its pride." [25]

Then, in 1912, Gourmont gave another definition in connection with a discussion of the role played by that movement in the *Mercure de France:*

But perhaps we should understand symbolism, just as I have always written and thought of it, as a very individualistic literature, very idealistic, in the strictly philosophical sense of the term, in which variety and liberty must correspond to personal visions of the world. In this sense, symbolism technically would be an expanded and sublime naturalism, which was rather well defined by

Zola's phrase: 'Nature seen through a temperament,' if we give the word nature its full significance: the entirety of life and the ideas which represent it.[26]

Thus Gourmont could abandon such interests as gave birth to *Phénissa* and the *Proses moroses*, the taste for the morbid and perverse, the precious style, without sacrificing his loyalty to principles of freedom of expression and integrity of art. For Gourmont's definitions of symbolism were much concerned with what he was *against*—all those considerations which, in his opinion, were not concerned with the direct and sincere expression of individual feelings and ideas. These views remained unchanged. Gourmont's conception of Symbolism was sufficiently broad to include many styles and attitudes, a Laforgue as well as a Mallarmé, a Verhaeren as well as a Verlaine, and it permitted Gourmont to develop and change considerably within its boundaries without actually breaking out. For there is no question but what he changed greatly in style, ideas, aesthetics, and even in philosophy between the early 1890's and 1900; but this he could do without rejecting Symbolism as he conceived it.

There were, however, fundamental changes in Gourmont's ideas of language and style which bore directly on his attitude toward Symbolism. The quoted definitions of Symbolism say nothing of the style usually associated with that movement, at least in its earlier stages. We do not find the customary emphasis on suggestion and evocation, the avoidance of direct statement, the conscious creation of mystery, the predominance of "le rêve," the concern for the musicality of words, and the use of "wavering rhythms" and incantation, in the effort, as Valéry said, to create a "state" in the mind of the reader. In his criticisms of contemporary writers Gourmont approved of these elements of the new poetry, and he exploited them extensively in his own early poetry, but he did not include them in his formal definitions, as did other Symbolists—Mallarmé, Verlaine, and Yeats, for example. Nevertheless, when he came to abandon them in favor of a new style—the direct, hard, concise, and concrete "imagistic" style—he was, in fact if not in theory, abandoning some of the distinguishing features of Symbolism as conceived by other practitioners.

Gourmont admitted his various contradictions, and he defended them in his preface to *La Culture des Idées* (1900): "I am not one of those who claim to have immutable ideas. Perhaps nobody is more changed than I. That is because successive meditations make me see things from a constantly renewed point of view, and I do not see why I should shut my eyes to those new viewpoints." Surely one must grant the right of a critic to change his mind, to develop and revise. Much of Gourmont's value derives from his capacity to reflect accurately the changes and developments of his time, to become "the critical consciousness of his generation," as Eliot puts it. But the cultivation of contradictions is another matter. As pointed out earlier, Gourmont felt that he "breathed more freely" in an atmosphere of contradiction, for it insured flexibility of mind and resistance to dogmatism. However, his contradictions were often more apparent than real, and when real, he usually applied himself to their resolution, to a new synthesis.[27] But this tendency is unquestionably related to what many critics have singled out as Gourmont's abiding weaknesses: a fundamental dilettantism, a facile skepticism which detracts from the intensity of his work and impoverishes his ideas, and a tendency to repeat himself unduly.[28] It is true that Gourmont echoed himself throughout his numerous articles and thus weakened the value of many of those pieces—perhaps the result of writing too much, too many "feuilletons" dashed off in haste perhaps to meet some deadline. Gourmont's forty-odd published volumes are too many, in view of what he had to say.

Gourmont's essays on individual poets of his time have, however, a lasting value. They contain perceptions and judgments which have lost none of their freshness in the last fifty years. But, because of their brevity, they are often frustrating and disappointing. Gourmont offered us

tantalizing fragments, provocative tidbits which he resolutely refused to develop. Although he was an "official"
critic of the Symbolist Movement, he never wrote a
searching or profound book about the *poetry* of the movement. In his *Livres des Masques* and volume four of
Promenades littéraires he gave shrewd but often disappointing accounts of individual writers, because he
would not dig deeply into his subject. Gourmont is usually
more impressive when making statements of principles or
dealing in general ideas than when elucidating a single
author. In some of his best criticism, the essay on Villiers
de l'Isle-Adam, for example, he quickly moved from the
text to the philosophy which lies behind it. Turnell is correct when he says that Gourmont wrote better about
other critics than about poetry, and that the best essays in
the *Promenades* are those concerned with the ideas and
practices of Renan, Rivarol, Sainte-Beuve, Brunetière,
and Lemaître. For in the last resort, as Turnell says,
Gourmont was true to "the French approach"—he was
"more interested in the movement of ideas behind the
poetry than in the poetry itself." [29] This is especially true of
the later Gourmont, who had moved away from the "intoxication of words" to seek out their history and meaning.
He became increasingly interested not only in the movement of ideas behind the poetry, but also in the complex relationship between the ideas and the poetry, and
in the problems posed by the mysterious process by which
sensation and idea become language. Thus, while we may
regret Gourmont's failure, or refusal, to discuss specific
works with greater thoroughness, it was that very prefer-
ence for general ideas that gave us his valuable studies
of the problems of style.

THERE HAS BEEN a tendency among some influential critics to think of Gourmont's theories of language solely in terms of his early writings, those stemming from his first enthusiasm for Symbolism, such as "L'Ivresse verbale," one of the essays in the *Idéalisme* collection. As a result, Gourmont has been placed in the "ultra-aesthetic" category and left there.[1] Such critics display either ignorance of or indifference to Gourmont's later and more important writings which represent, not a passing fancy, as does "L'Ivresse verbale," but the mature judgments which came to be Gourmont's final opinions on the subject of language.

In his early articles Gourmont proclaimed his love for the "personal esthetic" of words, their rarity and sonority —they are "perfume to our imaginative senses." He preferred words whose meanings were "closed" to him, imprecise words and "syllables of dreams"—"What music is comparable to the pure sonority of obscure words, o cyclamor?"[2] But Gourmont soon outgrew such tastes, the turning point coming in 1899, when he gathered together a number of articles on language and published them under the title of *L'Esthètique de la Langue française*. This work is concerned with such problems as "deformation" of language and the nature of clichés and metaphors. It retains but one aspect of Gourmont's earlier passion for words: verbal beauty. He no longer rhapsodizes on the beauty of words, however; he studies that beauty's source, its history and its enemies. Gone are the exotic, the bizarre, the foreign; the emphasis is now on *purity*.

> Esthetic of the French Language—that means examination of the conditions under which the French language must evolve in order to maintain its beauty, that is, its original purity. Having noted . . . the harm caused our language by the indiscriminate use of exotic or Greek words, of barbarous words of all origins and all makes, I was led to ponder my impressions and to discover that those intruders were ugly just as a faulty tint in a painting or a false note in a musical phrase is ugly.[3]

Gourmont wished to introduce a new principle into the study of languages, "the aesthetic principle," but terms like "beauty" and "purity" should not be interpreted too narrowly. One should not hesitate, Gourmont assures us, to bring science into literature or literature into science— the time of such "fine ignorance" is past. One should "gather into his mind all possible knowledge" and reject old forms of mental compartmentalization based on prejudice and ignorance.[4] These pronouncements reflect Gourmont's general interest in synthesizing seemingly contrary modes of intellectual activity. The *Physique de l'Amour*, for example, was written with the style (and often the imagination) of the novelist rather than of the conventional scientist. On the other hand, Gourmont's poetry (*Fleurs de Jadis*, *Dit des Arbres*, and *Simone*) is rich in scientific and especially botanical material. Imported words, however, are avoided in favor of "purely French" terms.

At about the same time (February 1899) Gourmont published an essay, "Du Style ou l'Ecriture," which was expanded a year later into *Le Problème du Style*. This essay was originally conceived as a reply to the popular writings of Antoine Albalat,[5] who advocated the learning of literary style through the diligent study and imitation of great writers. In this attack on Albalat we see the practical application of Gourmont's "scientific philosophy" and theories of artistic creation. One does not learn how to write or how to acquire a personal style by study and imitation:

> The true problem of style is a question of physiology. . . . We write, as we feel, as we think, with our entire body. The intelligence is only one of the modes of being of the sensibility, and not the most stable, still less the most voluntary.
>
> Style is to feel, to see, to think, and nothing more.
>
> Style is the product of the physiology, and one of the most constant, though dependent on the various vital functions.[6]

As opposed to Albalat's theories of imitation, Gourmont asserted that a writer merely must live and feel. If he is an intelligent and sensitive person, he will, after the manner of vertebrates, revolt against his milieu. He will interpret it according to his own sensibilities, and that interpretation will have value only if completely new in thought and style. As he lives, he must have a personal experience of the world; thus he must have, involuntarily, an original style. Gourmont grants that this process involves to some extent the necessity of imitation. After all, to live is to imitate, both because a general sensibility imposes itself upon all men of the same period and because a young writer can become "impregnated" by a work he has excessively admired. Furthermore, the imitation of subjects in art is to be expected. This is not only permissible but inevitable, for there are but few subjects in the world, and they are sure to be treated by many writers, each after his own fashion and in his own style. However, during the act of writing, one must never think of either his masters or of his own style. If he merely sees and feels, he will say something. Whether it will be interesting or not, effective or mediocre, is a matter of chance.

During the period of adolescence imitation is to be expected, indeed perhaps desired, but as a writer matures he must progressively disengage himself from his youthful admirations. He will become interesting only as he finds his own style: "Life is a process of sloughing-off. The proper end of a man's activity is to scour his personality, to cleanse it of all the stains deposited by education, to free it of all the imprints left by adolescent admirations." [7]

According to Gourmont's sensualist theories, the true problem of style becomes the problem of the interpenetration of the world of sensations and the world of words. There lies the great "mystery," for the two worlds are far apart, parallel, and communicate only by some sort of mysterious wireless.[8] As a rule, words and sensations are rarely and poorly in accord with one another. Potentially, however, every sensation is ambivalent, according to Gourmont's aesthetic. In the state of an image, a sensation represents at once reality and the state of the soul of its creator. The more an author is original, the more his sensibility is complex and the more complete will be the interpenetration of the external world and his temperament. Thus, both the critic and the poet, in judging the world or works of art by way of their personal temperaments, judge according to the most permanent of criteria. The intransigence of the sensibility leads it to give a logical and reliable response to those problems which bothered many literary schools of the nineteenth century, because the sensorial writer, both critic and poet, gathers under one principle the seemingly contradictory problems of "reality" and "ideality." For him, the material and the subjective world, all life and all sensation, have an absolute value. But it is essential that the creator approach life without intellectual or abstract preoccupations. He must above all see and feel, and write only after having lived. This principle, in whose name Gourmont proscribes from the domain of art all emotion born of the individual contemplator and not of the thing contemplated, is extremely important. It lies at base of all great art: "If, instead of sensations, of material memories, the brain retains only the imprint of an emotion, or if the perception of the senses is rapidly transformed into an abstract notion, or into an emotional idea, art is no longer possible, for there is no art but plastic art and the material has fled, leaving only its tracks along the way." [9]

Here Gourmont divides writers into two major types: the *visuals,* who retain a spectacle in the form of a relatively clear image and so tend to write in a concrete style, and the *emotives,* who remember only the emotion which a spectacle aroused in them and so tend to write in an abstract style. Of the two types, it is the visual who is more apt to be the true artist, for "the master faculty of style is the visual memory." However, "if, to the visual memory, the writer joins emotional memory, if he has the power, in evoking a material spectacle, of putting himself back into the exact emotional state which that spectacle aroused in him, he possesses, even unawares, all the art of writing." [10]

Concrete style, according to Gourmont, is one into which the entire sensibility has been incorporated and it is the only style which will produce art. In an abstract style the sensibility has not been assimilated into the language. This kind of style either does not permit art, or else it permits only a very vague sort of art, lacking in reality. On these grounds Gourmont ultimately came to oppose both theoretical idealism and theoretical realism in literature, because in both there is an abstract preoccupation which vitiates the evidence of the senses before it can be assimilated, before it can be incorporated into the subconscious and thence into language. Thus the writer who strives too consciously to represent things as he sees them will be the more incapable of doing so, because the intellectual effort on behalf of exactitude will dominate and corrupt the evidence of the senses. This was the plight of the Naturalists. Many Idealists (Gourmont called them "spiritualists") tried on the other hand to embellish life according to a previously established plan, but moral emotions born "à propos" of an object do not necessarily spring from the object itself. Such writers create only lifeless puppets. [11]

Just as art is thwarted by conscious literary theory, so it is incompatible with a moral or religious preoccupation.

Citing the "solitaries" of Port-Royal as examples, Gourmont explained that such people tend to be bad writers, because their sensibilities are channeled into their moral or religious activities, and not into their art. Their style is often abstract or sentimental, whereas that of "l'écrivain-artiste" almost never is. The true artist absorbs all his sensibility into his style and there remains little left over for everyday life and its passions: "Style is a specialization of the sensibility. . . . The more a writer approximates the artist, the less he is apt to cut a figure in the various manifestations of human activity." [12]

Gourmont expanded his "visual" and "emotive" types into two broad classifications of writers: the "sensorial" and the "ideo-emotive," or, in other words, the "plastic" and the "sentimental." According to the Gourmontian theory of language, the cycle of mental activity can be divided into three stages: first, the sensations, which are transformed into images (*mots-images*); second, images are transformed into ideas (*mots-idées*); third, ideas become emotions (*mots-sentiments*). The cycle then closes in action.[13] The literary sensibility is composed of the first two stages. It builds sensation into image and begins the process by which image is crystallized into an idea. This is the process of the sensorial writer—he creates directly out of his sensations. He deals with images which are the immediate product of those sensations: "An idea is only a stale sensation, an effaced image; to reason with ideas is to assemble and combine, into a labored mosaic, faded cubes which have become almost indistinguishable." For an idea to have color and life, it must have sprung from sensation, from an immediate image. Once cut off from the senses that created it, an idea becomes pure "parroting"—it becomes rhetorical and abstract. Furthermore, it is necessary for feeling to enter into the use and manipulation of ideas, said Gourmont, quoting Pascal: "Geometric propositions themselves become feelings." "The senses are the only doorway through which enters all that lives in the mind, the very notion of consciousness, the very feeling of personality. . . . The

logic of the eye and logic of each of the other senses
suffice to guide the mind. . . . One makes those marvelous constructions which seem to be purely intellectual
works and which, in reality, are the material work of the
senses and their organs—like the combs of bees with their
wax and honey." [14]

For this reason thinking by means of sensorial images
is much easier and more reliable than thinking by ideas.
"The sensation is used in all its verdure, the image in all
its vivacity." Here Gourmont quoted Hobbes in support:
"The imagination is sensation which is prolonged, but
weakened" (*Elementa Philosophiae*). This is what produces the "solidity" of the work of such philosophers as
Schopenhauer, Taine, and Nietzsche, as distinct from that
of abstract thinkers like Hegel and the "spiritualists."
"Philosophy, which passes popularly for the domain of
pure ideas (those chimaeras!), is lucid only when conceived and drawn up by sensorial writers." The Hegelians
are condemned as "idéo-émotifs" who do not recognize
that a doctrine is nothing but "the verbal translation of a
physiology." [15] Here Gourmont quotes Taine himself to
prove, contrary to the opinions of Albalat and Emile
Faguet, who considered Taine's style "artificial," that it
was in fact the product of his sensibility: "I ask pardon for
these metaphors [Taine wrote]; one gives the impression
of arranging his sentences, and *he is only recounting his
sensations*" (Gourmont's italics). [16] But Gourmont did
not content himself with merely quoting Taine; he devoted several pages to demonstrating the concreteness of
Taine's style, rich in sensual imagery. He pointed out that
Taine was unusual in that he possessed this style from
the time of his youth, whereas ordinarily a young man
rarely has an original "imaged" style. The artistic faculties,
Gourmont explained, being based on the "exercise of
sensation," cannot be anterior to sensation. The senses
are developed by the natural education given by life:
"A sensorial style, a style of images, is never precocious;
it develops in proportion as sensations accumulate in the
neural cells and make the archives of the memory denser,

richer, and more complex. . . . It is life, it is the habit of sensation which will create the stylistic image; but the grain, even at that indecisive period, manifests invincible tendencies. Taine's brain was, from his childhood, the brain of a visual and a sensorial." [17]

What Gourmont was principally concerned to combat here is the notion that such a style can be learned. Faguet had claimed that Taine's style was "a miracle of the will," and Gourmont, who opposed the belief of Mallarmé and Valéry that poetic language could be consciously "willed," was here opposing critics of prose style on the same grounds. He again quoted Taine, "One does not give himself his style; he receives it from the facts and deeds with which he is dealing." Gourmont said that this analysis is good, but incomplete. It should read, "One does not give himself his style; its form is determined by the structure of the brain, from which one receives the factual material with which he deals." [18]

Gourmont's theories brought him to a position directly opposite to the ideas so vehemently expressed in his earlier "L'Ivresse verbale." He came to disdain "stylists"—"les artisans du verbe." If, to write well, one must translate sensations, then authors who compose fancy phrases without having derived them from lived experience, or, as Gourmont expressed it elsewhere, without having transcribed an original idea resulting from an inner need for expression—such authors write badly, however graceful and charming their style.

Gourmont also took issue with Albalat on the question of the importance of subject matter in literature. Albalat claimed substance to be much less important than style—it is the manner of expression which creates the originality of the subject. Gourmont, reversing his earlier views, asserted that the substance has an "absolute importance." "Nothing dies faster than a style which is not supported by the solidity of strong thought. . . . As the thought has value, so the style has value: there is the principle." [19] Here Gourmont appears to contradict the opinion advanced in "Du Style ou de l'Ecriture," in which he affirmed that "all the elements of which style is composed are so many truths as useful and perhaps more precious to the human mind as those which comprise the substance of the subject." [20]

However, as is often the case with Gourmont's "contradictions," the disparity resides in the expression, not in the ideas. Just as Gourmont rejected the beautiful style that is not "lived," so he rejected the thought that is not sufficiently individual. The thought must be so well anchored in the author's physiology that it can be immediately translated into an original language. A bad style, as well as a style that is too *recherché*, indicates that an organic unity between the thought and the expression does not exist, that there is no "life" behind the words. Furthermore, there is a difference between "thought" and "subject," and since the number of subjects is limited but infinitely flexible, "the invention of themes is not of great interest in literature." But style (that is, "thought," for "thought" and "style" are inseparable) provides variety to the basic themes: "Everything would have been said in the first hundred years of literature, if man had not had style by which to diversify himself . . . But had there been in the world only one solitary theme, and it was Daphnis and Chloé, it would have been sufficient." [21]

Gourmont placed little importance on the subject as such, but in his criticism he continually stressed the need for unity of thought and style. He often reproached Hugo for seeking "effects," for sacrificing naturalness for verbal magnificence: "I cannot really like the style of writers whose thought I detest. I would go so far as to neglect completely those verses which do not contain some idea or true feeling: that is why there are so few pages of Victor Hugo that fully satisfy me." [22] He found in the work of Rostand the same grave shortcoming: "The poetry of M. Rostand lacks personality. It lacks thought, profundity." [23]

Does this mean, however, that Gourmont denied the possibility of verbal invention in literature? If one accepts the physiological determinism on which he based his theories of literary creation, it would seem that the problem of language is no longer a problem. Gourmont would appear to be contradicting himself in seeking fundamental principles of verbal invention—as in his discussion of metaphors and, above all, of the relationship between the particular fact and the general word in the realm of poetic expression. According to his belief that style is a specialization of the sensibility, language should correspond exactly to the thought being expressed. However, in an essay on "la Rhétorique," Gourmont explained that the theoretical study of language is nevertheless necessary because thought and expression are never completely one. Wondering what is the cause of continual disharmony between these two reciprocal activities, Gourmont suggested: "Words, outside of proper nouns and certain rare, highly systematized, common nouns, correspond to general ideas, whereas the writer very often claims to express unusual or at least characteristic ideas." [24]

This contradiction can be better understood in the light of what Gourmont said about "the rhetoric of nuances" in another essay. After stating the problem, "It is a question of putting the world of ideas into accord with the world of words," Gourmont explained that, at first contact, the rapport between the two worlds is perfect. In the subconscious, when the sensation is transformed into *mots-images*, it seems that the words completely cover the idea. At the moment of inspiration the writer is perfectly comprehensible and clear—at least to himself. But he wishes to communicate his thought, to transpose it into signs intelligible to others. Then he finds that the interdependence of the world of sensations and the world of words is far from being perfect; he feels that "in sum, words and sensations are in harmony only very rarely and very poorly." [25] For the reader and critic the work of a great writer is always somewhat mysterious precisely because the creator cannot express perfectly what he experiences. Feeling the disparity between sensation and expression, between the experience, which is concrete, and the word, which is abstract, the writer does the only thing he can do: he seeks the most exact word, that is, the nuance. Furthermore, even if style is a mode of being, a way of reacting to experience and is thus inviolable, there is nonetheless a "science of words" which, if it cannot be "taught," can be clarified in its essential aspects. For in the ideas of Gourmont this distinction is evident: along with the natural style, a phenomenon of physiological origins, there exists an "art of expression" that can be imposed on style and learned only by writers of innate aptitude. But in the last analysis, it remains "exterior," a work of education.

It was with the true artist, however, that Gourmont was concerned, "l'écrivain-artiste" whose use of language is not to be confused with the comparatively modern "art of writing." Gourmont's conception of language, as H. V. Routh points out, is of primitive antiquity, "a fact of life like mobility, pervading all the processes of consciousness, a phenomenon of biological significance." [26] But it must be added that the modern writer possesses a quality unknown to the primitive literary mind—the art of "lying." For to Gourmont, the creation of a metaphor is derived from the modern capacity for feigning. He explained that the most elementary form of visual imagination is the simple comparison, the simile. It antedates the metaphor, the comparison which lacks one of its terms or has blended two terms into one. There are no metaphors in Homer and they are very rare in the *Chanson de Roland*, and that, Gourmont asserted, is the incontestable sign of primitiveness. To the relatively rude sensibility of a Homer, sensations are successive, hence language is successive. He describes a fact, then another fact, comparing one to the other as an analogy, as a simple simile. He is exact, through an inability to "lie"; he describes his impressions one after another, as they arrive, without confusion. A modern writer, on the other hand, is a master of an artistic prevarication:

Flaubert, who has a capacity for lying and therefore an infinite capacity for art, is not being exact when he writes: "The elephants . . . the rams of their breast-plates like the prows of warships, were cleaving their cohorts; they flowed back together in great waves." He blends the images so well only because he has seen them at a single glance (elephants and cohorts, ships and waves). What he gives us is no longer two designs symmetrically superimposed, but the confusion, visually absurd and artistically admirable, of a doubled and muddled sensation.[27]

Therefore, when M. Albalat gives Homer as the supreme model for imitation, he gives bad advice, principally because, apart from the fact that conscious imitation is bad, the Homeric style is a representative of a primitive manner of seeing life and is in "an absolute contradiction with our 'synesthetic' tendencies." It is impossible for us to dissociate the double or triple images born simultaneously in our tumultuous minds, just as it was impossible for Homer to make an association which we now make spontaneously and in spite of ourselves. We no longer feel the need to establish the exact fact we wish to record, and then to relate another analogous fact which explains, reinforces, or extends the first fact. Modern art comes from enunciating, at one stroke, the two facts, "interlaced with the degree of ability of which each talent is capable." "The metaphor is indispensable to us; those who, because of the constitution of their brains, are inept at creating new metaphors, use those that are current. Every cliché was once a new metaphor and survives as a banal metaphor. The cliché is a coin tossed into circulation; the metaphor is the first copy of that coin." [28]

Modern literary art is based, then, on the metaphor and the metaphor is based on the visual imagination. Gourmont gave great importance to this faculty, exalting the visual over the other senses. It is only rarely that the name of a flower, a food, or a material can be translated in the sensibility by impressions of odor, flavor, or touch, though it may be a normal occurrence in certain individuals. And there are those sensorials, Gourmont admitted, in whose complex sensibilities the idea of love arouses a tumult of "hallucinations." But on the whole "the quality of the imaged style corresponds to the quality of the eye, to the quality of the visual memory, and also to the quality of the verbal memory." [29]

ii

Commonplace as some of Gourmont's ideas might appear today, their influence on English and American writers of the time can hardly be overestimated. Middleton Murry's *The Problem of Style*, for example, shows unmistakable evidence of Gourmont's influence, though that indebtedness is not always acknowledged. In fact, Eric Bentley, in his introduction to *The Importance of Scrutiny*, says that Murry's *Problem of Style* contains many applications of Gourmont's ideas, but that "none too much is added." Murry does appear to echo Gourmont in many places, and he quotes some of Gourmont's own sources: Stendhal, Baudelaire, and Flaubert. In a few places he borrows Gourmont's phrases, as when he refers to Racine's language as "abstract and frigid, almost diplomatic" (p. 138), an expression obviously taken from Gourmont's statement that Racine expressed extreme passions in "un style abstrait, glacé, et diplomatique." [30] On other occasions he gives Gourmont as a source, as in the beginning pages of his *Problem of Style*, where he discusses the vagueness of critical terms, using Gourmont's analysis of "decadence" and his distinction between literary and social decadence.

Both books on style are based on the belief that language and style are "organic," and Murry echoes Gourmont to the effect that an individual way of seeing and feeling compels an individual way of using language. [31] A "true idiosyncrasy of style," Murry tells us, is "the result of an author's compelling language to conform to his mode of experience, and . . . a false idiosyncrasy is produced when the vital reference of language to this mode is lost, or not yet found." Furthermore, the most valuable quality of writing is "concreteness"; and concreteness produces a "solid" style, that is, "complete economy, complete precision," in which "the piece of writing has been completely ejected from the writer's mind." This latter statement seems to be Murry's version of Gourmont's idea that in a good style the writer incorporates his entire sensibility into his language. Murry also affirms Gourmont's idea that a contrived and *outré style* is not peculiar solely to youthful strivings for originality, but to mature writers also. "The test of a true idiosyncrasy of style is that we should feel it to be necessary and inevitable; in it we should be able to catch an immediate reference back to a whole mode of feeling that is consistent with itself."

Although Murry reveals considerable indebtedness, he does not always merely echo Gourmont, and it is misleading to say that "none too much is added" to Gourmont's ideas. He is highly critical, for example, of Gourmont's contention that the power to visualize is essential to a worthy style. This, Murry avers, is a "half-truth." The truth is "not so much that an author must himself possess a great power of visualising—even where his gift is mainly descriptive—as that he must possess the power of making his readers see things on occasions." These are two very different faculties, Murry asserts. Indeed, the precise visual image plays a very small part in a metaphor; rather, "perceived quality in one kind of existence is transferred to define a quality in another kind of existence." It is not so much a precise visual image that is evoked as the "evocation of just so much visual background as will enable us to feel the quality that is being transferred." Murry agrees that great writing depends on a wide range of sensuous experience, refined into a system of "emotional conviction." However, the apprehension of the quality of life as a whole, the power to discern the universal in the particular, and to make the particular a symbol of the universal—this ability is not derived merely from sensuous experience, but rather from "emotional contemplation." But sensuous experience is nevertheless necessary for the complete expression of this contemplative experience. Thus a writer needs an accumulation of vivid sensuous experiences, of "perceived qualities with little fragments of context."

In his conception of imagery Murry is probably closer to Baudelaire and such Symbolist writers as Mallarmé and Valéry than he is to Gourmont. For to Murry the concrete image is "made to arise not before the vision but before the imagination." One does not actually *see* the image—"images are bathed in the virtue of the immaterial condition they define." And while the writer looks for "similitudes in other spheres of existence for the thing that he is describing . . . giving a physical turn to the spiritual," what actually happens is that "the physical is taken up into the spiritual," and not vice-versa.

This corresponds rather closely to Mallarmé's view of language. Mallarmé believed that in poetry the purpose of words is not to enhance our sense-consciousness of the object. The purpose of the object is served when, on the contrary, it has, by the words it suggests to the creator, referred us to the abstracted Idea of itself. As Norman Suckling points out, the images in Mallarmé's poems are not the usual "visual images"—they are more akin to "intellectual images." Mallarmé's "clotted imagery," which suggests mixed metaphor, is not incongruous because no material illustration is intended and because the Ideas of disparate objects may well be not so mutually contradictory as their occurrence would be in material juxtaposition. Mallarmé aimed at intellectual images, or, as he termed them, *"notions pures."* In ordinary language words fade out before the object, whereas in poetic language, according to Mallarmé, it is the object in its material or practical concreteness which disappears. In contrast to Gourmont's emphasis on the concrete object and the immediate sensation produced by the sensuous apprehension of that object, Mallarmé emphasized the primacy of the "pure idea": "What good would be the marvelous transposing of a fact of nature into its vibrant near-disappearance in the play of words, were it not that from it might emanate, without constraint of a close or concrete reference, the pure idea?" The word has meaning only if it releases us from the object that it names. It must remove the "presence" or "concrete recall" of the object; it effects a separation only to retain the *idea*. In its authentic poetic function, the word has a destructive, not a representational, function. It causes the object to disappear; it annihilates it. The result is, as Suckling says, that the evocation of *visual* images becomes, in Mallarmé's aesthetic, "the function of words *least* proper to poetry." [32]

The poetry of both Mallarmé and Valéry demonstrates the belief that poetic intensity is most surely achieved, and sentimentality most surely avoided, "by using no word that directly describes a feeling or proceeds directly from an affective state." [33] This "disinterested contemplation" and Murry's "emotional contemplation" are based on the conviction that in the poetic treatment of feelings and ideas, the language is not destined to arouse the same reactions as would be aroused if the subject matter were treated other than poetically. The feelings and ideas have been purified of their concrete attributes and "taken up into the spiritual," as Murry puts it. They have been transmuted, in terms of language, into autotelic and intrinsically valuable "states of mind." And this is achieved by imagery derived from all the senses, of which the visual is but one, and not the most important, as Gourmont would have it.

Gourmont would probably see Murry's conception of imagery and his "emotional contemplation" as tending toward the stage of *mots-idées* and *mots-sentiments*, images which give only a faded version of the vital sensations that created them. In his aversion to all abstraction, Gourmont would counsel the rendering, through the precise use of words, of the sensation itself, fresh and still intact. The closest he came to Murry's "emotional contemplation" was his observation, previously cited, that "if he has the power, in evoking the material spectacle, to put himself back into the emotional state which that spectacle aroused in him, he possesses, even unawares, all the art of writing."

iii

The problem of Flaubert's style is one that has received a generous share of critical attention, and it is to be expected that Gourmont would devote many pages of the *Problème du Style* to the Norman master whose works he considered the perfect fusion of thought, sensibility, and language. But what complicates the study of Flaubert's style—a problem that apparently disturbed Gourmont not at all—was the fact that Flaubert possessed at different periods in his career strikingly different styles. Thibaudet, for example, distinguishes at least three: Flaubert's first works up to *Madame Bovary*; then the style of his great novels, *Bovary* to *Bouvard et Pécuchet*; and the style of his *Correspondence*. The definitive Flaubertian style is of course the second—though his *Correspondence* has found many admirers—and there is much evidence to suggest that it was a "willed" style, one that Flaubert worked hard and long to disengage from his other two styles. And one might well ask, did it disengage itself, or was it Flaubert who disengaged it? Here is Gourmont's view of the problem:

> Like all the writers of his time Flaubert was initially influenced by Chateaubriand; that is neither miraculous nor very important. Emerging from any other school, Flaubert would inevitably have become what he was, himself. Life is a process of sloughing-off. The proper end of man's activities is to scour his personality, to cleanse it of all the stains deposited by education, to free it of all imprints left by adolescent admirations. A time comes when the scoured coin is clean and shining with its own metal. But to use another image, I think of the sloughing-off of wine which, freed from its disturbed particles, its vain fumes, its false colors, one day becomes gay with all its grace, proud with all its strength, limpid and smiling like a new rose. Since Flaubert is one of the most profoundly personal writers that ever existed, one of those who may be read most clearly through the lace of style, it is easy to follow in his work the progressive sloughing-off of the man. To do

that, one must read successively *Madame Bovary, L'Education sentimentale, Bouvard et Pécuchet*; only in this last
book is the work completed, only there does the man's
genius appear in all its transparent beauty. . . . The only
books are those where a writer has recounted himself by
recounting the manners of his contemporaries, their
dreams, their vanities, their lives and their follies. What
are the descriptions of *Salammbô* and their long cadenced
phrases compared with the brief notations and resumés
of *Bouvard et Pécuchet*, that book which is comparable
only with *Don Quixote?* [34]

But a close study of Flaubert's letters, wherein he recounts in painful detail his struggles to find the apt
expression, *le mot juste*, suggests that his style was much
more a matter of contingency than Gourmont grants. It
is quite probable that Flaubert's ultimate style was
neither inherent nor inevitable; rather, as Thibaudet
says, "it is apparent that he has extracted his style from
his nature by an effort of discipline and an act of will.
It is also apparent that it could have been otherwise."
Every sentence of Flaubert's style implies a tension and a
choice. Those are the keys to his entire work—tension and
choice, movement and will. Also, the "sloughing off" that
Gourmont discusses and that continues from *Novembre*
to *Bouvard*—does it not, Thibaudet asks, exceed its intended aim? For after Flaubert became "as limpid and
smiling as a new rose," he developed the transparency of
onion skin, then weakened and died.[35] Indeed, few
readers today share Gourmont's enthusiasm for *Bouvard*,
and only *Madame Bovary* can be meaningfully compared
with *Don Quixote*.

The problem of the necessity or contingency of style can
scarcely be resolved to anyone's satisfaction—linked as it
is with the general problem of free-will and determinism,
which one can argue indefinitely. However, while Gourmont's solution seems somewhat limited and his sensual-
ism and determinism somewhat summary, his *Problème
du Style* "raised a hare that has never stopped running."
His provocative approach to the problem—the attempt

to synthesize psychology, physiology, and aesthetics—was welcomed with enthusiasm by many English and American writers of the subsequent generation, and an elaboration of his ideas can be seen in the complex theories of contemporary aestheticians like I. A. Richards and Suzanne Langer.[36]

5 GOURMONT AND THE ANGLO-AMERICANS

ALTHOUGH Gourmont was to become a leading model and inspiration for the American Imagist poets, he did not have to wait on that movement for his introduction to American readers. His work was well known to certain cosmopolitan literary journalists of the turn-of-the-century. It was probably James Huneker who, by featuring him in his *Mlle New York* in 1895, first introduced Gourmont into the United States and made him known during the 'nineties. Two years later Huneker reviewed the *Livres des Masques* ("Notes," *Nation*, March 1897) and protested that Gourmont was a writer unjustly ignored in this country. The same year he made the Frenchman's acquaintance and established friendly relations with him that were to last several years. The first really substantial study to appear in America was Huneker's "Remy de Gourmont" in the *New York Sun*, June 14, 1900, and from that time on Huneker's essays were studded with quotations from his French friend. *Unicorns* (1917) included "Remy de Gourmont: His Ideas. The Colour of His Mind," a rapid, head-spinning tour of Gourmont's ideas and assertions, rather bewilderingly written, though in a tone of great admiration and homage. In remembrance of the *Promenades littéraires*, he entitled one of his collections of articles *Promenades of an Impressionist*.[1]

After Huneker there were others, namely Vance Thompson, Benjamin de Casseres, and Burton Rascoe, who wrote of Gourmont in a journalistic spirit, though, in

Taupin's words, "with no other aim than to cultivate their readers." Taupin observes that "a critic of the rank of Vance Thompson gives several pages out of *Livres des Masques* in his *French Portraits* (1900), without changing a word in them and without mentioning Remy de Gourmont," and concludes that "it merely proves that the manner of Remy de Gourmont could appeal to the public as early as 1900." [2]

The main wave of interest in Gourmont, however, reached America about 1915 and lasted into the 'twenties, a period of considerable vogue of *Les Chevaux de Diomède, Lettres à l'Amazone,* and *La Dissociation des Idées* among younger readers, and of the *Problème du Style* among students of writing. Gourmont's admirers may not have been numerous, but they were intensely devoted; indeed, they were often given to outbursts of high praise that verged on the ridiculous. Huneker had made great claims for Gourmont's brilliance and importance, but he supported his assertions with evidence and cogent reasoning. Benjamin de Casseres, on the other hand, used Gourmont to display his own talents, and treated the serious Frenchman with a mad rhetoric, summing up many of Gourmont's important views in a few flashy phrases. [3] Pound and Aldington hailed him as one of the most original and erudite men of the age, and Eliot attributed to him the "intelligence of an Aristotle." But John Macy topped them all with his insistence that "Remy de Gourmont is not a great poet nor a great novelist, but the greatest critic that has ever been born, even in France where critics are wont to be born." [4]

Gourmont seemed to inspire this sort of extreme reaction in his followers and to evoke cheers and praises which seem extravagant today. However, to many young readers of that time—and it was to the young that Gourmont made his greatest appeal—he seemed the archetype of the free spirit. Aldington and Huneker appreciated his individualism and made use of his example in their own individualistic propaganda; [5] that is, in 1915 writers saw in Gourmont a fine reflection of their own aspirations. He especially pleased them because the freedom that he fought for was not really anarchical, though it appeared so to his more conservative opponents. As Aldington wrote in *The Little Review* (1915), "He has an influence, especially over the younger and more adventuresome spirits, which few writers today possess," and as Pound wrote to Sarah Perkins Cope (April 22, 1934), "My generation needed Remy de Gourmont."

So translations of his works, mostly by Pound and Aldington, began to appear frequently in literary magazines on both sides of the Atlantic—the *Egoist* and *Criterion* in England, the *Little Review* and the *Dial* in America, with a special tribute paid in the "Remy de Gourmont Number" of the *Little Review* (February–March 1919), to which Pound, Aldington, and others contributed.[6] Translations of Gourmont were not confined to the little magazines, however. As early as 1912 Arthur Ransome's translation of *Une Nuit au Luxembourg* found a popular audience, and during the 'twenties the rest of his novels were translated, along with numerous renderings of his plays and poetry. In 1921 William Aspenwall Bradley published his "authorized translation" of Gourmont's essays in a volume entitled *Decadence and Other Essays on the Culture of Ideas*. In 1926 Ezra Pound translated *The Natural Philosophy of Love* (*Physique de l'Amour*), with a postscript. In 1928 Aldington produced his large, two-volume *Remy de Gourmont: Selections from all his works*, and in 1931 he brought out his translation of *Letters to the Amazon*.[7]

Of all the lively periodicals in England and America, the *Egoist* showed the greatest enthusiasm for French poetry. The first issue (January 1, 1914) contained several articles on France, including a continuation of a translation of *Les Chevaux de Diomède*, begun earlier in *The New Freewoman* (the *Egoist's* predecessor). The April 1 issue contained more French material, with the name of Remy de Gourmont appearing most often. Aldington observed that the work of Gourmont had been the object of more commentaries in the *Egoist* than in any other

English periodical because, he believed, "many young people fond of literature felt that Gourmont was the most attractive literary artist living in France at that time" (*Egoist*, March 16, 1914). And from 1915 on, the *Egoist* published considerable poetry in the original French by Gourmont and his contemporaries.

ii

Gourmont has often been considered one of the leaders of the *vers-libriste* movement, and to a certain extent he was; but his views on free verse were not always clearly understood. Actually he advocated a very limited freedom and warned against its indiscriminate use. Nevertheless, he was taken for a champion of emancipated verse forms and was hailed by exponents of new movements in both England and America, and especially by F. S. Flint, a leader of V*ers-libristes* in England. A minor English poet, critic, and a close student of French literature and the current "isms," F. S. Flint helped launch the English "infatuation" for France. As a theorist, he gave the Imagists direction in their attacks on traditional poetry. As a poet, he gave them models for their own creative efforts,[8] and he played an important part in introducing Gourmont's ideas to his fellow poets. Writing in the *New Age* as early as July 8, 1909, Flint hailed Gourmont as a "liberator" and gave an enthusiastic survey (Flint was invariably enthusiastic when writing of French poetry) of Gourmont's principal works and theories: "It is impossible to pass through these [Gourmont's] books without feeling that new eyes and a new understanding are being given to me; old images and metaphors are broken up and made useless; associations that have grown mouldy are crumbled; and fresh with the dew of a new morning the earth again awaits the re-born artist." He went on to praise Gourmont's pagan freedom, his ability to fuse literature and science, his "creative skepticism," his perpetual youth, vitality, and joyous sensuality.

Flint wrote many articles praising Gourmont's individualism and nonconformism, which he felt to be very necessary but lacking in England at that time, but he was principally concerned with propagating Gourmont's theory of "non-rimed cadence." This theory, which was held in high esteem by English *vers-libristes,* advanced a belief in the physiological basis of cadence in prose; it asserted that rhythm is modeled on the nature and intensity of the emotion felt by the individual. Furthermore, of all the Imagists, Flint most closely followed Gourmont's dictum that "there should arise, at almost regular intervals, a full and complete line, which reassures the ear and guides the rhythm."

As a matter of fact, Gourmont took a rather conservative view of free verse. He did not advocate its practice: "It requires a great deal of talent to write a good poem in free verse; it requires perhaps even more to read it properly and to feel it." He preferred to a thorough-going free verse what he called "le vers libéré," a "liberated" verse which had a more solid basis in traditional rhythm and metre. In the complete context of his statement he said:

> Liberated verse, while remaining faithful to the metre, plays tricks with metre and toys with the mutes, dropping them and calling them back at will. As has already been said, it is not necessary that a line have a dozen real syllables; it must appear to have them. But the common measure being the real metre, there should arise, at almost regular intervals, a full and complete line, which reassures the ear and guides the rhythm. There is no poetry without rhythm, nor rhythm without metre.[9]

Gourmont added that it is only in the sense of a modified free verse, the *vers libéré* in which a certain stability of rhythm and metre is retained, that the term can be associated with the Symbolist movement. A close connection between free verse and Symbolism, in his opinion, would have seriously impeded the evolution of that movement.

iii

T. E. Hulme, usually considered one of the founders of Imagism,[10] reflected many of Gourmont's ideas but rarely mentioned the Frenchman by name. Herbert Read, in his introduction to his edition of Hulme's *Notes on Language and Style* (University of Washington Chapbooks, 1929), states, "It is not claimed that Hulme's theories are in any way original. They owe a good deal, I think, to Remy de Gourmont's *Problème du Style*, and perhaps a little to Jules de Gaultier, the author of *Le Bovarysme*." René Taupin believes that it is "quite certain" that Hulme formulated his ideas of imagery in language with the aid of *Problème du Style*, and he adds that one needs only to read the chapter on "Romanticism and Classicism" in Hulme's *Speculations* to be convinced. Taupin sees both Hulme and Gourmont as "educators" and points of departure for other writers. Both were aware of the "simple fact" that the faculty of vision is the basis of all literary art—an idea, Taupin points out, that was influential for many years until "supplemented and rectified" by Middleton Murry and I. A. Richards.[11]

Hulme agreed fundamentally with Gourmont as to what was needed to rejuvenate a languishing literature. At the time when the Imagists launched their movement in England, poetry was being written in what the young poets considered a "worn-out language," lacking in emotional richness and sincerity—a tired poetic diction sanctioned by long use by the great poets of the preceding century. This imitativeness had resulted in a merely verbal poetry in which it was permissible "to pad out lines with words which were useless, and hence harmful, to the sense of the poem, provided that those words were agreeable to the ear habituated to the sounds and rhythms of the Victorian poets." [12] The Imagists, largely under the leadership of Hulme and Ford Madox Ford, directed their best efforts toward the rectification of these "insincere" and "lazy" habits. They saw the problem mainly in terms of style; they believed that style was the key to the sincerity of the poet.[13] Aldington, in an almost exact quote from Gourmont, described style as "thinking, perceiving, and expressing oneself precisely and individually." Amy Lowell, in her preface to an anthology of Imagist poetry (1915), quoted Gourmont at length and demanded that poetry be written in words that are exact—not in approximate or merely decorative words. That same year Miss Lowell published *Six French Poets,* in which she devoted a chapter to an appreciative survey of Gourmont's poetry.[14]

Gourmont's great contribution to the study of style was his taking the problem out of the realm of signs and pure verbalism and recasting it in terms of modern psychology and (updating Buffon's celebrated phrase: "Style is the man") modern physiology. Gourmont had emphasized that "we write as we feel, as we think, with our entire body," [15] and Hulme echoed him. We should realize, said Hulme, that "all our analogies spiritual and intellectual are derived from purely physical acts. . . . All poetry is an affair of the body—that is, to be real, it must affect body." [16]

Both Hulme and Gourmont believed that poetry stems from the entire sensibility and that each word should be a *seen* image: the visual image is the basis of poetic creation. Hulme compares worn images and clichés, in Gourmont's terms, with old coins that have lost their lustre through long use. Gourmont had opined that old metaphors are like "médailles usées"—"with obverse and reverse sides so effaced that the most tyrannical imagination can no longer animate them." He added that "nevertheless many who prefer to use these coins also make use of their eyes in order to classify the worn verbal riches stored in their memory." [17] Hulme's version of this conception was that "every word in the language originates as a *live* metaphor, but gradually of course all visual meaning goes out of them and they become kind of counters." He added that visual sensation is necessary to revivify the worn images.[18]

Gourmont insisted that words tend to evolve toward abstraction, that is, toward death, and that the progress of language therefore depends on the creation, if not of new words, at least of new images. Moreover, the creation of new images is essential to exactitude of expression and to conformity with the initial vision (*Prob.,* 53). Hulme put it this way:

You could define art, then, as a passionate desire for
accuracy, and the essentially aesthetic emotion as the
excitement which is generated by direct communication.
Ordinary language communicates nothing of the individuality and freshness of things. . . . The element in it
[aesthetic emotion] which will be found in the rest of art
is not the accidental fact that imagery conveys over an
actually felt visual sensation, but the actual character of
that communication, the fact that it hands you over the
sensation as directly as possible, attempts to get it over
bodily with all the qualities it possessed for you when you
experienced it.[19]

The following two quotes from *Speculations* also appear
to bear the Gourmont stamp:

It [poetic language] is not a counter language, but a visual
concrete one. It is a compromise for language of intuition
which would hand over sensations bodily. It always endeavors to arrest you, and to make you continuously see a
physical thing, to prevent your gliding through an abstract
process. It chooses fresh epithets and fresh metaphors, not
so much because they are new, and we are tired of the old,
but because the old cease to convey a physical thing and
become abstract counters. . . . Visual meanings can only
be transferred by the new bowl of metaphor. . . . Images
in verse are not mere decoration, but the very essence of an
intuitive language.[20]

Metaphors soon run their course and die. But it is necessary to remember that when they were first used by the
poets who created them they were used for the purpose of
conveying over a vividly felt actual sensation. . . . the
reality of sensation experienced.[21]

It is by the number of his images, Hulme said, that
one can measure the sincerity of a poet.[22] He presumably
meant the number of fresh and original images, for he
went on to assert that a freshness of expression is necessary to create between the poet and his reader a *direct*
communication, which is the primary source of aesthetic
pleasure. He further agreed with Gourmont that original-

ity and sincerity in literature are derived not from other works so much as from life itself, that the substance of a poem must be concentrated in a few concise images, and that the subject in art is not as important as form and style.

In matters of inspiration, sincerity, exactitude, and literary beauty, Hulme and Gourmont both based their theories on the same basic conception: the "doctrine of the image," the absolute importance of the concrete rendering of sensation. A major difference between the two men is that Gourmont demanded that a writer be capable of incorporating into his style "all the sensibility he has at his disposal," including the emotion as well as the reason, which is only the "sensibilité cristallisée"; whereas Hulme was inclined to reduce poetry to a simple vehicle of sensations, to a purely descriptive art.

The Imagists owed an immense intellectual debt to Gourmont, and they were able to repay him in a very substantial fashion during the war years 1914–15. The war had so disrupted normal publishing practices in France that Gourmont was left with virtually no income. Many writers on both sides of the Atlantic did what they could to aid him—they tried to have his articles published, for pay, in American periodicals. Pound and Aldington had some success in finding remunerative outlets for their French friend's work, and Aldington enlisted on Gourmont's behalf the very considerable influence and wealth of Amy Lowell.[23]

In the fall of 1914 Aldington wrote to Miss Lowell pointing out that Gourmont was being ruined by the war. She agreed to help. Aldington had sent money in payment for some translations he had made of Gourmont's works; he was trying to sell more translations in the United States and to get a Gourmont poem to submit to *Poetry*. Aldington asked Miss Lowell to recommend Gourmont's poems to Harriet Monroe, editor of *Poetry*, and to help find Gourmont a position as Paris correspondent for an American periodical. He also suggested that she might advance some money, about two hundred dollars, on shares which Gourmont held in an Anglo-Egyptian Land Bank.

While not sharing Aldington's devotion to the Frenchman, Miss Lowell knew Gourmont's work well and admired him. On hearing of Gourmont's plight she sent him two hundred dollars as an anonymous gift, and then wrote to Aldington refusing the bank shares and pointing out that "This seems a very little sum to pay for all the inspiration and knowledge I have derived from his writings." She then proceeded to find Gourmont a job: he was to write six articles on "present conditions in France," for which the *New Republic* would pay him two cents a word—hardly a princely sum. She asked Aldington to relay the offer to Gourmont and apologized for the accompanying proviso: nothing "very French" that the magazine would "consider unadvisable to publish." She was sure that the cash and the chance to reach an American audience would outweigh the expected indignation, and she asked Aldington to assume the role of go-between and translator, which he did without remuneration. Later Gourmont sent Miss Lowell a contribution to her collection of manuscripts with an inscription expressing his gratitude.

As it so happened, Gourmont's articles caused considerable trouble. The *New Republic* was disappointed in the articles (they reflected all too clearly Gourmont's ill health and fatigue) and refused to publish them. The result was an exceedingly heated letter from Aldington to the editor of the *New Republic*, which prompted a complaint from the editor to Miss Lowell who was obliged to assume an embarrassing role as peace-maker. All was solved, however, when the *Boston Transcript* bought the entire series of six articles, thus saving both the *New Republic* and Gourmont's American well-wishers from a most awkward situation.

This happened during the last year of Gourmont's life (he died September 27, 1915). His American friends had been able to ease some of the distress of his final months and had expressed, in a way that must have been most gratifying to the ailing and depressed Gourmont, their loyalty and gratitude to him for his timely and much needed assistance in their own poetic wars.

iv

It was in the work of the two major graduates of the Imagist school, Pound and Eliot, that Gourmont's ideas on criticism and style produced the most fruitful results. Although both writers, especially Eliot, tended eventually to abandon the Frenchman in the mature development of their art, there is no question but that Gourmont was one of the decisive influences in the formation of their early attitudes. It is clear, in the many articles that Pound wrote on Gourmont, that his appreciation of the Frenchman took two distinct forms. First, Pound was impressed by Gourmont as a *man*, as a living symbol of the artist devoted to freedom and originality, to the highest integrity in art and to liberty in matters of personal conduct —all of which Pound found most encouraging in his personal war with Anglo-Saxon morality and mediocrity in literature. He was also highly appreciative of Gourmont's role as guide and inspiration of young writers. In *Poetry* (January 1916) he wrote: "I think I do not write for myself alone when I say no other Frenchman could have died leaving so personal a sense of loss in the minds of many young men who had never laid eyes on him. . . . M. de Gourmont was indubitably 'of the young' in the sense that his mind had not lost its vigor, that he was alive to contemporary impressions. . . . He had never lost touch with the men born ten or twenty years after he was."

Pound had once dreamed of establishing an international literary review representing works from New York, London, and Paris. He had written to Gourmont, among others, asking for support. Gourmont offered contributions, but the project never materialized. Later Pound wrote in the *Little Review* that if Gourmont had lived

he would have been included among "our own associates," and that his last letter concerning the proposed
review was consequently of an "entirely personal interest"
to friends. He added that it was of more general interest
when one considered how few disinterested and friendly
critics there were in America at that time, and that
the words of Gourmont were not without some light to
bring to the subject of Franco-American literary relations.
Here is Gourmont's letter to Pound, which Pound printed
in its original French in the *Little Review* (December,
1917):

Dear Sir,

It was with great pleasure that I read your long letter,
which revealed to me so clearly the need for a review
bringing together the efforts of the Americans and the
French. For that reason I will serve you to the extent of my
abilities. I do not believe that I can do very much. I am
in poor health and am extremely fatigued. I could give
you only a few short things, some token pieces rather than
finished pages, but I will do my best. I hope that you will
succeed in putting this little project on its feet, and that
you will find among us some useful concourse. Obviously
if we can bring the Americans to a fuller appreciation of
the true French literature and above all not to confuse it
with the mediocrity of much current output, it would be a
most happy consequence. Whether the Americans are
capable of sufficient liberty of mind to read, without
being shocked, my own books, for example, is very doubt-
ful; and such acceptance would require a long work of
preparation. But why not undertake it? In all countries
there is a core of good minds, of free minds. We must give
them something in contrast to the insipidity of the magazines, something which will give them confidence in themselves and be a source of support for them. As you say, it
will be necessary, as a beginning, to bring them to respect
French individualism, the sense of freedom that some
among us possess to an extremely high degree. They
understand this in theology, why would they not understand it in art, in poetry, in literature, in philosophy? We
must make them see—if they do not see it already—that
French individualism can, when necessary, bend itself to

the strictest of disciplines. To conquer America is no doubt not your only aim. The aim of the *Mercure* has been to permit those who are worthy of it to write frankly what they think—the sole pleasure of a writer. That aim should also be your own.

> *Yours devotedly,*
> *Remy de Gourmont*

Besides admiring Gourmont the man, Pound was influenced by both Gourmont's stylistic theories and his poetic practice. He was influenced first of all by the Symbolist poetry of the early Gourmont, and then by the Imagist theories of style of the later Gourmont. In the first instance Pound, who did not like all of Gourmont's poetry (he rejected *Simone* as imitative), thought very highly of the verse deriving from Gourmont's study of the Latin Middle Ages. Speaking of *Le Latin mystique* he says that Gourmont "laid before his few readers a great amount of forgotten beauty," and he goes on to say that the influence of Latin verse appears in Gourmont's own poetry, especially in the *Litanies de la Rose:* "the curious evocational form, the curious repetitions, the personal sweeping rhythms, are made wholly his own." [24]

There is some question, however, as to the extent to which French Symbolism influenced Pound's poetry. Stanley Coffman insists that "for Pound, the French poets were an inspiration, a confirmation, but not a source of theory," that "he admired their technical proficiency, but he was uninterested in the philosophy of Symbolism, and he ignored those poets and that verse which most closely approximated a Symbolist pattern." [25] There is evidence from Pound himself to support this view. In a letter Pound wrote to René Taupin (May 1928) he insisted that he was "oriented" before knowing the modern French poets and that the Symbolists had no direct influence on his own work. Regarding the "symbol" he makes the amazing statement that he had never read "the ideas of the symbolists on that subject" and that he could recall "nothing from Gourmont on the subject of 'symbol.'" [26]

Also in tacit support of Coffman's view is the observation by Taupin that "it is the mind of Gourmont rather than the creations of that mind which Pound likes to set up as an example." Taupin quotes Pound, "As you read de Gourmont's work it is not any particular phrase, poem or essay that holds you so much as a continuing sense of intelligence in the mind of the writer." [27] And in *The Literary Essays of Ezra Pound* we see a similar observation: "But there is nothing more unsatisfactory than saying that Gourmont 'had such and such ideas' or held 'such and such views'; the thing is that he held ideas, intuitions, perceptions in a certain personal exquisite manner. In a criticism of him, 'criticism' being an over-violent word, in, let us say, an indication of him, one wants merely to show that one has himself made certain dissociations."

Pound made it clear, then, that in citing Gourmont and other "recognized and civilized" men of letters, he was borrowing their prestige to combat American "imbecility," and that, as Coffman suggests, he was not the least interested in Symbolist ideas. Nevertheless, while Pound may not have cared for Symbolist poetry in general, there is abundant evidence that he has not only studied, and recommended that others study, Gourmont's Symbolist verse, but that he incorporated many of its devices into his own work. Furthermore, his frequent citing of Gourmont's opinions suggests that the matter as well as the manner of Gourmont's thought was of importance to him.

Speaking of Gourmont's *Litanies de la Rose*, Pound states that one of the great gifts of Symbolism was the doctrine that the poet should *suggest*, not present. Under the influence of the medieval *sequaires*, Pound adds, Gourmont found his own form in poetry: "an effective indirectness. The procession of all beautiful women moves before one in the *Litanies de la Rose*; and the rhythm is incomparable. It is not a poem to lie on the page, it must come to life in audition, or in the finer audition which one may have in imagining sound. One must 'hear' it, in one way or another, and out of that intoxication comes beauty." [28] He compares Gourmont's Symbolist art with the exquisite creations of Japan. "I do not think it possible to overemphasize Gourmont's sense of beauty. The mist clings to the lacquer. His spirit was the spirit of Omakitsu; his *pays natal* was near the peach-blossom-fountain of the untranslatable poem." [29]

It was from Gourmont's poetry that Pound derived the idea of the necessity of strong cadence, well marked by rhythmic elements expressed in cadence at the outset and repeated in the body of the poem—the idea that rhythm is scansion operated by the respiratory system, itself subject directly to the emotions. He was impressed by Gourmont's notion of an "absolute rhythm" corresponding exactly to the emotion or the "color of an emotion" which the poet endeavors to express. "I believe in an absolute rhythm. I believe that every emotion and every phrase has some toneless phrase, some rhythm-phrase to express it." [30] As Hugh Kenner points out, Pound was clearly aware that the belief in absolute rhythm leads into "deeper issues," that "as a structural relation . . . 'absolute rhythm' provides at once a psychological and an objective correlative of emotions and shades of emotion transcending both exegesis and vocabulary." [31]

This theory is the counterpart, in terms of rhythm, of the doctrine of the image. It demands of the poet in matters of cadence the same qualities of invention and exactitude as the creation of new analogies in matters of language and style. This rhythmic power, along with a mastery of verbal melody, Pound found in the poetry of Gourmont. He advised the study of the *Litanies* and the *Fleurs de Jadis* as models and stimulants in the feeling and creating of new and expressive rhythms.

Critics have found it interesting to compare some of Pound's poems in *Ripostes* (1912) with Gourmont's work. Mossop sees similarities in the color imagery and rhythmical effects of Pound's "Apparuit" and the *Litanies*, and Taupin believes the "Martagon" section of *Fleurs de Jadis* to be the model for Pound's "Midonz" section of

"The Alchemist." Here are the sections of the two poems in question:

Martagon dont les têtes se dressent par centaines,
monstre odorante, hydre azurée,

Martagon dont le front porte un turban de pourpre,

Martagon dont les yeux sont jaunes, lys byzantin,
joie des empereurs décadents, fleur
favorite des alcôves, parfums des Saintes Images,

Martagons, multiples Martagons, je vous préfère à
d'autres monstres dont je pourrais dire le nom, fleurs
tréspassées, fleurs de jadis.

Midonz, with the gold of the sun, the leaf of the poplar,
*   by the light of the amber,*

Midonz, daughter of the sun, shaft of the tree, silver of the
*   leaf, light of the yellow of the amber,*

Midonz, gift of the God, gift of the light, gift of the sun,
*   Give light to the metal.*

Coffman rejects the notion that any direct influence exists between the two poems. He points out that Pound's concept of free verse was never a copy of the French, "the difference lying partly in his emphasis upon a quantitative measure that the French language does not permit." In a footnote Coffman admits Pound's "early admiration of the rhythms of De Gourmont's *Livres des Litanies*," but, regarding the possible influence of that work on "The Alchemist," maintains that Pound's poem "seems to have been written before Pound was closely acquainted with French poetry."

Ripostes, however, appeared in 1912, and in the same year Pound published his praise of Gourmont's "absolute rhythm" corresponding exactly to the emotion which it endeavors to express ("Prolegomena," *The Poetry Review*, February 1912); and the following year saw the

publication of "The Approach to Paris: Remy de Gourmont" (*New Age*, September 1913). Furthermore, Flint,
who is credited with introducing Gourmont's work to
Pound, had been praising Gourmont's rhythmical powers
since 1909, so it seems possible that the poems of
Riposte were written under some influence of Gourmont.
Moreover, "emphasis upon a quantitative measure" not-
withstanding, there is a remarkable resemblance between
the "Martagon" and "Midonz" poems.

However, while the relations between the *Litanies* and
the poems in *Ripostes* might suggest as much affinity as
direct influence, the debt of Pound's *Hugh Selwyn
Mauberley* to the *Litanies* has been convincingly established by J. J. Espey in his *Ezra Pound's Mauberley: A
Study in Composition*. Espey confesses that much of his
study falls under the heading of "source-hunting," but he
defends this practice in the special case of Pound: "That
the tracing of a source may substitute an appearance of
understanding for genuine penetration is perfectly possible, but so long as one distinguishes between the casual
source—the discovery of which is a harmless enough
pastime—and the source that genuinely informs a piece of
writing, the method has its own objective values. For an
artist of the order of Pound, himself so frequently the
Ph.D. *manqué* in both prose and poetry, it can prove
peculiarly revealing."

Espey feels that Gourmont's work does indeed provide
meaningful sources for Pound's *Mauberley*, and he devotes a chapter entitled "Physique de l'Amour" to exploring that relationship. He finds in Pound's verse references not only to Gourmont's poetry but also to the
erotic stories, *Histoires magiques*, and to the *Physique de
l'Amour*:

> The similarity between the range of Gourmont's work and
> Pound's is striking. An interest in Provençal poetry, in the
> later Latin poets, in a studied eroticism, and willingness
> to generalize from sometimes slender evidence or even
> from a single fixed point characterize both men. The
> Gourmont used by Eliot is a somewhat different Gourmont

from the author of the *Epilogues* and *Promenades Littéraires*, from the Gourmont of *Physique de l'Amour* with its vivid account of the virgin mole's flight before inflamed pursuer, from the Gourmont of the cheerfully erotic collection of stories, *Couleurs*, in which Gourmont, carrying on the vowel-color symbolism of Rimbaud and René Ghil, equates colors with feminine types, each of whom finds her own shade of amorous fulfillment. It is this second who attracted Pound.[32]

This is somewhat misleading, for while Eliot appears to have successfully avoided the *Physique de l'Amour* and its passionate moles, he was fully alive to the *Promenades littéraires* as well as to Gourmont's other studies in criticism and style. Moreover, Pound showed considerable awareness and appreciation of those works which Eliot admired, *Le Problème du Style* and the *Livres des Masques*. However, as far as those works which influenced Pound in the composition of *Mauberley* are concerned, Espey is certainly correct. The harmonious sounds and rhythms of the *Litanies*, along with much of Gourmont's sex-flowers-music symbolism, found their way into Pound's own work. As Espey says, "One recognizes immediately the reflection of Gourmont, in tone, in the flowers, in the rhetorical questions, and one suspects that somewhere in the aesthetic bouquet must lurk a specifically sexual reference beyond the mention of 'amour.' " [33]

Espey stresses Pound's enthusiastic approval of Gourmont's emphasis on the body: "In contradiction to [Pound wrote], in wholly antipodal distinction from, Henry James, Gourmont was an artist of the nude." Pound appreciated not only the "scientific" studies of Gourmont's later period but even more the perverse creations of "decadent" Symbolist erotica. Espey finds evidence of the rich, sensual imagery of the eye, fingers, mouth, of colors, perfumes, and musical references symbolic of sexual activity and climax; and he studies Pound's development of Gourmont's theories of sexuality as it appears in Pound's appended note to his translation of the *Physique de l'Amour*. Espey lines up an impressive array

of sometimes obvious and sometimes subtle indica-
tions of Gourmont's influence, and concludes by quoting
Pound's discussion of Gourmont's role: "In, let us say,
an indication of Gourmont, one wants merely to show
that one has oneself made certain dissociations; as here,
between the aesthetic receptivity of tactile and magnetic
values, of the perception of beauty in these relationships,
and the conception of love, passion, emotion as an intellectual instigation."

Here, Espey asserts, is *Mauberley*'s base, expressed
through Pound's own dissociation of ideas in Gourmont's
work: "The dissociation is precisely the dissociation
Pound makes between the muses of Gourmont and James;
it is the structural dissociation made between the two
parts of *Hugh Selwyn Mauberley* as a composition; it is
the dissociation made between Pound, the poet of 'love,
passion, emotion as an intellectual instigation,' and
Mauberley, the poet of 'aesthetic receptivity of tactile
and magnetic values, of the perception of beauty in these
relationships.' " [34]

Ultimately, however, Pound came to realize the contradiction between the long sonorous cadences of the
Litanies and the early prose poems, and the new Imagist
technique. He had found in Gourmont's early verse the
art of manipulating "the homogeneous units" of thought
and feeling within a stanza, and of introducing a syn-
tactical and verbal parallelism which guides the rhythm.
But these were verbal effects, aimed at suggestion and
evocation, and so had little to do with the precepts in the
later *Problème du Style*, with its Imagist emphasis on the
direct in poetry. So, in addition to quoting Gourmont on
questions of rhythm, Pound came to defend the technique
of "direct treatment" and to advocate the use of a sensorial and concrete style. He rejected not only the abstract,
but the alliance of the abstract and the concrete: "Don't
use an expression like 'dim lands of peace,' it spoils the
image"; that is, it mixes two categories. This fault, Pound
adds, stems from the fact that the writer has not understood that "the natural object is always the adequate

symbol." [35] Further reflections of the later Gourmont appear in letters from Pound to Harriet Monroe: "There's no use in a strong impulse if it is all or nearly all lost in a bungling transmission of the impulse intact," and "Language is made out of concrete things. General expressions in non-concrete terms are a laziness; they are talk, not art, not creation. They are a reaction of things on the writer, not a creative act *by* the writer" (January 1915).[36]

In 1915 Pound expressed his admiration for Gourmont's "prose sonnets" to the Amazone (scattered through the *Lettres à l'Amazone*), praising in particular their impersonal and dryly scientific tone; and in the literary movement, Vorticism (ca. 1914), he placed great emphasis on the "primary form" of art, that is, sensation as the primary material of art. But as time went on Pound had less to say of Gourmont's ideas on style; rather, in his growing discontent with Anglo-Saxon civilization, he wrote articles praising French culture and citing Gourmont as the shining example of the cultivated, independent, and honest intellect.

It is feasible to maintain, as Mossop does, that Pound was the link between the language reforms attempted by Hulme and those achieved by Eliot; and that of the three writers Pound probably owed the least to Gourmont but was more outspoken in praise of the Frenchman's influence. Hulme stressed Gourmont's criticism, Pound his poetry; but the influence on Pound, in Mossop's opinion, was much less tangible. Mossop feels that, in the last analysis, it was probably Gourmont's personality, his mind and manner of thought, and his attitude toward art and life that chiefly impressed Pound. Coffman tends to agree with Mossop and believes that the French poets were an inspiration and confirmation rather than a source of theory. Espey's book, however, published a few years later than Coffman's, convincingly establishes many examples of the direct influence of Gourmont's writings on Pound's which Pound did not acknowledge and the earlier studies did not observe. A close examination of the works of Pound and Gourmont makes it clear Espey is correct.

One difficulty in reading both Pound and Gourmont is the fact that most of their major ideas have been so completely assimilated into modern thinking as to appear commonplace. What Eliot said of Pound, in his introduction to the *Literary Essays of Ezra Pound*, could also be said of Gourmont: "Much of the *permanence* of Pound's criticism is due simply to his having seen so clearly what needed to be said at a particular time; his occupation with his own moment and its needs has led him to say many things which are of permanent value, but the value of which may not be immediately appreciated by later readers who lack the sense of historical situation."

Both were notably forthright critics, and by today's standards they appear to have exaggerated the importance of some principles and authors, and to have unjustly depreciated others. But both have enriched criticism by their interpretations of neglected works and by their rehabilitation of misjudged authors. Above all, they both had great influence on younger writers, through their devotion to the art of good writing, and in their exemplary resistance to the sterilizing forces of convention.

v

Of the many English and American writers of the early twentieth century who were close students of French literature, T. S. Eliot probably knew best and made the most significant use of Gourmont's work. There were four great French influences on Eliot's early criticism —Charles Maurras, Julien Benda, Baudelaire, and Gourmont—but Gourmont seems to have contributed the most positive theories of criticism.[37] Both Eliot and Gourmont insisted that criticism is, or should be, "creative." They rejected the popular idea that criticism is parasitic, living on the work of others.

They agreed on many basic questions of aesthetics, on the "integrity of poetry" and its independence of moral, political, and social concerns, and on the need for a new approach to poetic language. This was of course the early Eliot, who, from roughly 1917 to 1927, saw in Gourmont the "perfect critic." The recurrence of Gourmont's name in Eliot's many contributions to the *Egoist* and *Criterion*, the use of epigraphs from Gourmont as section-headings in *The Sacred Wood*, and his frequent references to Gourmont in the *Selected Essays* make the matter of indebtedness clear. In his preface to the 1928 edition of *The Sacred Wood* Eliot says of his early years: "At that time I was much stimulated and much helped by the critical writings of Remy de Gourmont. I acknowledge that influence and am grateful for it." He goes on to describe Gourmont as "the critical conscience of his generation" and as having, of all modern critics, "most of the general intelligence of Aristotle," combining to a remarkable degree "sensitiveness, erudition, sense of fact and sense of history, and generalizing power." Eliot found in Gourmont a provocative predecessor in the development of his own concept of sensibility as fundamental to both critical and creative activity and in his campaign to rejuvenate prevailing literary practice. However, it is clear that Eliot used Gourmont only as a point of departure; his ultimate ideas differ considerably from those of the Frenchman. Nevertheless, it can be shown that he drew certain "principles of order" from Gourmont's often ironic, contradictory, and skeptical writings.

Like Gourmont, Eliot was convinced of the crucial role of physiology in artistic creation. Both men were concerned to know how sensation is transformed into language, how intelligence achieves a work of art. To accomplish this, Gourmont, as we have seen, probed deeply into contemporary studies in psychology and physiology, ultimately arriving at the conviction that thought is the product of the sensibility, that the intelligence is closely connected to the sensibility and consequently to the body, and that literary style is therefore a product of the total physiology.[38]

When we turn to Eliot's view of the role of sensibility in the creative process, we see what appears to be a direct

borrowing from Gourmont, especially as regards the necessity of "leaving the original acute impression unchanged":

> We assume the gift of a superior sensibility, and for sensi-
> bility wide and profound reading does not mean merely a
> more extended pasture. There is not merely an increase of
> understanding, leaving the original acute impression un-
> changed. The new impressions modify the impression re-
> ceived from the objects already known. An impression
> needs to be constantly refreshed by new impressions in
> order that it may persist at all; it needs to take its place in
> a system of impressions. And this system tends to become
> articulate in a generalized statement of literary beauty.[39]

Eliot also echoes Gourmont in his own conception of
the physical basis of language and the importance of
metaphor:

> All thought and all language is based ultimately upon a
> few simple movements.* Metaphor is not something ap-
> plied externally for the adornment of style, it is the life of
> style, of language . . . we are dependent upon metaphor
> for even the abstractest thinking . . . The healthy meta-
> phor adds to the strength; it makes available some of that
> physical source of energy upon which the life of language
> depends.
>   * All this matter of cliché and the metaphor has been
> much more ably put in Remy de Gourmont's *Problème du
> Style*. [Eliot's footnote] [40]

It is in Eliot's essays on Renaissance dramatists that
we see the most rigorous application of Gourmont's principles to English poets. Not only in his choice of words
and phrases but by means of direct reference to the
authority of Gourmont, Eliot acknowledges his debt. Indeed, these essays are a far more thorough demonstration
of Gourmont's ideas in actual practice than Gourmont
ever made himself. The French critic lavished much
thought and evidence on the development of his critical
tools, but did not allow himself to use them fully, con-
fining himself to brief and often brilliant observations,
which, however, were not worked out in their full im-

plications. In the actual performance of criticism, Eliot
is often a more satisfying writer.

In his study of Massinger, for example, Eliot established
his mode of approach by describing the period of
Massinger, Webster, Middleton, and Donne as possessing
a language evidencing "a very high development of the
senses . . . a period when the intellect was immediately
at the tips of the senses. Sensation became word and word
was sensation." Massinger's verse, however, suffers from
"cerebral anemia": "To say that an involved style is
necessarily a bad style would be preposterous. But such a
style should follow the involutions of a mode of perceiving, registering, and digesting impressions which is also
involved. It is to be feared that the feeling of Massinger
is simple and overlaid with received ideas." Or, as Gourmont would say, Massinger's style remained on the level of
the "mots-idées" which were not the direct product of the
first stage of the creative process, the "mots-images" or
concrete sensations. Eliot goes on to say that Massinger's
works had the "highest degree of verbal excellence compatible with the most rudimentary development of the
senses." However, Massinger dealt not with emotions but
with "social abstractions of emotions . . . He was not
guided by direct communications with the nerves." [41]

Eliot then introduces Gourmont. "In the fine pages
which Remy de Gourmont devotes to Flaubert in his
Problème du Style, the great critic declares: 'Life is a
process of sloughing-off. The proper end of man's activities is to scour his personality, to wash from it all the
stains deposited by education, to free it of all the imprints
left by adolescent admirations.' and again: 'Flaubert incorporated his entire sensibility into his works. . . . Outside of his books, wherein he transfused himself, drop by
drop to the very dregs, he is not very interesting.' " [42]
Eliot declares that Shakespeare, Jonson, Marlowe, and
Keats, to varying degrees, "transfused themselves drop by
drop." Massinger, on the other hand, failed to do so; and
so, while he was "a brilliant master of technique, he was
not, in this profound sense, an artist." [43] Eliot's criticism

here is identical with Gourmont's reservations about the followers of Hugo, "les artisans du verbe," who did not qualify as "écrivains-artistes."

In his essay on "The Metaphysical Poets" Eliot pursues his early practice of applying Gourmont's words to English writers. He says of Jonson and Chapman, for example, that they "incorporated their erudition into their sensibility: their mode of feeling was directly and freshly altered by their reading and thought. In Chapman especially there is a direct sensuous apprehension of thought, or a recreation of thought into feeling, which is exactly what we find in Donne." [44] At a glance this appears to be pure Gourmont, but in fact it contains certain inversions of thought peculiar to Eliot. Eliot sees his writers as incorporating their erudition into their sensibility. Gourmont would say that their erudition was by an aspect of sensibility—an idea, a thought, is a form of sensation. When Eliot speaks of "a direct sensuous apprehension of thought," he is speaking pure Gourmont, but when he speaks of "a recreation of thought into feeling," he is reversing the order of events, as conceived by Gourmont in his three-stage theory of creation. Not that Gourmont would necessarily disapprove of Eliot's version, for the end result would be the same. This reverse process is also evident in Eliot's remarks about Laforgue, Corbière, and Baudelaire: "They have the same essential quality of transmuting ideas into sensations, of transforming an observation into a state of mind." [45] Gourmont would say that an idea, in so far as it is fresh and living, *is* a sensation. The problem, for Gourmont, is not one of transmuting an idea into a sensation, but rather of transmuting that idea, which is but a faded sensation, into language, into words capable of conveying the original feeling which lies at the base of the idea. That is the problem of style. However, the two critics are in essential agreement that ideas, to become material for art, must regain, or possess, the quality of sensual images or sensations.

It seems most probable that Eliot's well-known

phrase, "the dissociation of sensibility," originated in his reading of Gourmont. Although the term "sensibility" was current in French literature before Gourmont began using it, it was very likely Gourmont who, in giving the word special importance by founding it on a relatively well worked-out physiological theory of style, impressed it upon the minds of his Anglo-American readers. Furthermore, it was in certain key passages in one of Gourmont's best-known essays that "sensibility" is used in connection with the word "dissociate." In his "La Sensibilité de Jules Laforgue," Gourmont said that Laforgue's intelligence "was closely connected with his sensibility," adding that "all original intelligences are thus formed, the expression of physiology." But in the process of living one acquires "the faculty of dissociating his intelligence from his sensibility." This happens, sooner or later, by the acquisition of a new faculty, skepticism. Laforgue died before having reached this stage, and so he had passed his life in "watching the perpetual battle taking place within him between the intelligence and the sensibility, and that gave us the most beautiful, the most lively works." [46]

Eliot has made an interesting—and to many minds highly debatable—use of this idea when he transferred Gourmont's analysis of the mental processes of the individual to the study of English literary history.[47] That is, the unified sensibility that Gourmont had found in Laforgue, Eliot found in the England of the early seventeenth century. The skepticism which would have led, had Laforgue lived longer, to the dissociation of his sensibility and his intelligence receives its parallel in Eliot's "something which had happened to the mind of England between the time of Donne or Lord Herbert of Cherbury and the time of Tennyson and Browning." [48] In Gourmont's terminology, this would mean that English poetry proceeded from the period of *"mots-images"* (Donne, Herbert, Marvell) to one of *"mots-idées"* (Milton and Dryden). With the coming of "the sentimental age"— the second effect, according to Eliot, of the seventeenth-century dissociation of sensibility—it reached the period of *"mots-sentiments"* (Collins to Tennyson). F. W. Bateson believes that, while Eliot does not in this case use Gourmont's actual words, the general debt is "sufficiently clear." [49] He observes that the very vagueness and imprecision of the term "sensibility" enabled it to serve as an agent of unification of the diverse Anglo-American avant-gardes of the 1920's—the "senses" meant concrete objective fact to the Imagists, whereas they meant "instincts" to Joyce and Lawrence.

T. S. Eliot has made extensive use of the "dissociation of sensibility" concept. It became for him a criterion for evaluating the achievement of contemporary poets as well as a means of interpreting literary movements. For example, one can see a clear reflection of the Laforgue essay in Eliot's early criticism of the poetry of Marianne Moore: "Miss Moore is utterly intellectual, but not abstract; the word never parts from the feeling; her ideas, imageless, remain quite personal. Even in Laforgue there are unassimilated fragments of metaphysics and, on the other hand, of sentiment floating about; I will not assert that Miss Moore is as interesting in herself as Laforgue, but the fusion of thought and feeling is perhaps more complete." [50]

However, as suggested earlier, the relationship between Eliot and Gourmont was not entirely one of harmonious rapport. For example, in that complex problem which has commanded the attention of many modern theorists— the role of the subconscious in creative activity— we see a principal difference between Eliot and Gourmont. Whereas Eliot shows a great awareness of the function of sub-rational faculties in his insistence on the identity of thought and sensation, he does not give this conception the extreme emphasis that Gourmont did. Gourmont was very distrustful of the role of the conscious intellect in the creative process. To him it was useful only as final ordering agent *after* the process of inspiration and creation was nearly complete; otherwise its "interference" could be most harmful. Eliot, however, despite his emphasis on the primacy of the sensibility, did not trust it enough to leave it to its own autonomous resources: "There is a great deal, in the writing of poetry, which must be conscious and deliberate. In fact, the bad poet is usually unconscious where he ought to be conscious, and conscious where he ought to be unconscious. Both errors tend to make him 'personal.' " [51]

When Eliot agrees with Gourmont that there is a role to be played by the subconscious, he does not mean that the sensibility is to be given free rein. In his essay on Dante, where he defends the possibility of a philosophical poetry against Valéry's confinement of poetry to a "state of mind," Eliot uses, as an epigraph to that essay, a quotation from Charles Maurras: "The sensibility, saved from itself and brought into order, has become a principle of perfection." [52] Gourmont would not grant that the sensibility must be saved from itself. Indeed, it is the sensibility that "saves" the rational intellect, by preventing it from withering away in sterile isolation. The intellect is, in Gourmont's final analysis, only "crystallization of the sensibility." [53] But apart from this difference of opinion on the role of the subconscious, Eliot and Gourmont remain in essential agreement—"impressions" are the basis of literary activity, and literary judgment consists in "articulating" these impressions into "a generalized statement of literary beauty."

Eliot and Gourmont shared a distrust of the dogmatic critic who poses a rule or gratuitously affirms a value judgment. The work of such a critic is "incomplete"; he should elucidate in such a way as to permit the reader to form his own correct judgments. Gourmont said of the "hierarchical" system of official criticism, "It has a solid and serious air; [but] it is arbitrary, since esthetic or moral judgments are only generalized sensations." Eliot expands and deepens this concept: "True generalization is not something superimposed upon an accumulation of perceptions; the perceptions do not, in a really appreciative mind, accumulate as a mass, but form themselves as a structure; and criticism is the statement in language of this structure; it is a development of the sensibility." [54]

Here Eliot is speaking of the relation between "appreciation" and "intellectual criticism." He affirms that bad
criticism is nothing but the expression of emotion, and
he borrows Gourmont's examples of "emotional" people:
stockbrokers, politicians, and men of science. Eliot believed that in the dogmatic or lazy mind "comparison is
supplied by judgment, analysis by appreciation. . . . If
the critic has performed his laboratory work well, his
understanding will be evidence of appreciation; but his
work is by the intelligence not the emotions." [55] And he
agreed with Gourmont that Aristotle is the perfect fusion
of intellect and sensibility; Aristotle is "an eternal example
—not of laws, or even of method, for there is no method
except to be very intelligent, but of intelligence itself
swiftly operating the analysis of sensation to the point of
principle and definition." [56]

In his discussion of "The Perfect Critic," Eliot begins
one section with an epigraph from Gourmont's *Problème
du Style*: "The writer with an abstract style is almost
always as sentimentalist, at least a sensitive [*un sensitif*].
The artist-writer is almost never a sentimentalist and very
rarely a sensitive." [57] Although this passage would seem to
apply to the preceding section of *The Sacred Wood*, in
which Arthur Symons is condemned as a "sentimentalist"
in criticism, it serves here to introduce Eliot's views on
abstract and concrete styles. An abstraction, according to
Eliot, is "a meaning which cannot be grasped by appeal
to any of the senses." He goes on to explain that in
recent decades words have become increasingly indefinite
—they are losing their concreteness. With the proliferation
of knowledge, the same words are used with such widely
differing meanings that one is not sure what he is talking
about. "When we don't know what we are talking about,
or don't know enough, we tend to substitute emotions
for thoughts. However, not only all knowledge, but all
feeling is in perception." A literary critic, he adds, "should
have no emotions except those immediately provoked by
a work of art." [58]

Gourmont, in the complete context of the quoted epigraph, had explained that the artist-writer is almost never a "sentimental" and very rarely a "sensitif" because, according to his conception of style, the good writer incorporates all his sensibility into his style and has little left over for life's passions. "The one takes a ready-made phrase or makes up a facile one in which, deceived by his own emotions, he thinks he sees an emotive value; the other, with words that are merely handfuls of clay, constructs the limbs of his work and erects a statue which, whether beautiful or ugly, heavy or winged, will nevertheless retain in its attitude something of the life which animated the hands that shaped it." [59]

Gourmont pointed out that the "vulgar" person, whether reader or writer, will respond more fully to a banal phrase than to an original phrase. There is a vast difference between the reader who draws his emotion from the very substance of his reading and one who responds to his reading only in proportion as he can relate it to his own life, to his own fears and hopes: "Whoever tastes the literary beauty of a sermon of Bossuet cannot be touched by it religiously, and whoever cries over the death of Ophelia has no esthetic sense." The emotional writer, incapable of incorporating his sensibility into original stylistic formations, chooses those phrases which, having moved him in his own reading, he believes must surely move his readers in the same way. The result is abstraction and cliché.

In "Tradition and the Individual Talent" Eliot takes up this idea and greatly extends it. He agrees with Gourmont that "the effect of a work of art upon the person who enjoys it is an experience different in kind from any experience not of art." But he makes a fine distinction—the artistic experience is composed of two elements: emotions and feelings. The experience may be composed of one emotion or a combination of several emotions; and various feelings, "inhering for the writer in particular words or phrases or images, may be added to compose the final result." Furthermore, "great poetry may be made without the direct use of any emotion whatever: composed out of feelings solely." It is evident in this distinction between emotions and feelings, in this essay and others where the terms appear, that Eliot is using the latter word in the sense of "sensation," in a manner comparable to Gourmont's. In fact, "feelings," "impressions," and "sensations" all seem to be used interchangeably, at least in Eliot's early writing. Similarly, he will occasionally substitute "mind" for "sensibility." In a passage previously quoted, Eliot referred to the sensibility's receiving and assimilating various impressions. In "Tradition and the Individual Talent" he adds that "the poet's mind is in fact a receptacle for seizing and storing up numberless feelings, phrases, images, which remain there until all the particles which can unite to form a new compound are present together." Emotions, it would seem, are valid in literature only in so far as they derive from, find an "objective correlative" in, these concrete feelings and sensations, which take the form of specific words and images within the context of the work itself. But there are many impressions and experiences, which are important for the individual, both the writer and reader, that have no place in the poetry or the aesthetic experience, just as there are experiences, quite negligible for the individual, that are essential to poetry.[60]

In his insistence on the absence of "personality" in good poetry, Eliot might seem to be at odds with Gourmont, whose subjectivism placed great stress on individualism and originality in literature. Gourmont maintained that one should live and feel before writing, and that his style should be unique, the product of his individual sensibility. However, as he explained in his defense of impressionism, the good writer, either critic or poet, in plumbing the depths of his personal sensibility for his language and ideas, is in fact drawing on the accumulated feelings, attitudes, and experiences of his generation, of which he is but one concrete manifestation.[61] Believing, with Eliot, in a "generalized sensibility" or consciousness peculiar to each generation, Gourmont, for all his emphasis on the individual, was not as far from Eliot as it might seem. Both critics held that the superior writer subordinates the idiosyncratic and strictly personal to the demands of his medium. Gourmont granted that the artist was in fact the representative of his "caste" and the servant, to great extent, of its inherited ideals. Eliot, more conservative, granted that "to conform merely would be for the new work not really to conform at all; it would not be new, and would therefore not be a work of art . . . We say: it appears to conform and is perhaps individual, or it appears individual, and may conform; but we are hardly likely to find that it is one and not the other." [62]

Although the differences between Gourmont and Eliot appear to be mainly of degree rather than of kind, yet they are differences. Just as Eliot is less hostile to the intervention of the conscious intellect in the creative process than was Gourmont, so he is *more* hostile to the inclusion of emotion and personality. "Poetry," says Eliot, "is not a turning loose of emotion, but an escape from emotion; it is not the expression of personality, but an escape from personality." [63] Gourmont's version was somewhat different: "Personality does not consist, for a writer, in appearing on stage at an inopportune moment. . . . Personality as I understand it is nothing more than the very condition of originality; it has no need of being displayed." [64] He was far more willing to admit both emotion and personality, providing that they were expressed in a fresh and effective manner, that is, in a style deriving from concrete sensation and suggesting a degree of novelty. So it is on this point that Gourmont and Eliot part company. Eliot says, "One error, in fact, of eccentricity in poetry is to seek for new human emotions to express; and in this search for novelty in the wrong place it discovers the perverse. The business of the poet is not to find new emotions, but to use the ordinary ones and, in working them up into poetry, to express feelings which are not in actual emotions at all. And emotions which he has never experienced will serve his turn as well as those familiar to him." [65]

The first part of this passage treads squarely on Gour-

mont's toes. The searching for novelty and discovering
the perverse fits the early Gourmont exactly, but he did
eventually succeed in working free, though not completely, from this tendency. But the last part of the quotation agrees with one of Gourmont's early statements. He
had given the idea definite form in his *Livres des Masques*
(1896): "The equivalence of sensations is certain and the
horrors of fear can be told better by those who imagine
them than by those who feel them."

However, this involves Gourmont in something of a
contradiction. He was highly suspicious of the use in
literature of emotions not actually experienced; he feared
that it would result in artificiality and empty rhetoric—
mere verbalism lacking in the feel of life. In his early years
he seemed undecided about the relative importance of
creative imagination and concrete experience, but by the
turn of the century and the writing of his works on language and style, Gourmont, perhaps because of the
manifest rhetorical emptiness of much prevailing poetry,
came out strongly for concreteness of experience as a
necessary counter-balance to an overemphasis on verbal
invention. In any event, he would certainly have been in
sympathy with the immediate objective of Eliot's pronouncements: that of refuting the "emotion recollected
in tranquility" formula of poetic composition. He would
for the most part agree with Eliot that "it is neither emotion, nor recollection, nor, without distortion of meaning,
tranquillity. It is a concentration, and a new thing resulting from the concentration, of a very great number of
experiences which to the practical and active person
would not seem to be experiences at all; it is a concentration which does not happen consciously or of delibera-
tion." Recollectors of emotion in tranquillity would fall
into Gourmont's category of "idéo-émotifs," for whom
concrete sensorial images had faded into the past, leaving
only the abstract husks of feeling.

To clarify his belief that "the poet has, not a 'personality' to express, but a particular medium, which is only a
medium and not a personality, in which impressions and

experiences combine in peculiar and unexpected ways,"
Eliot has recourse to his well-known analogy of the poet's
mind as a neutral catalytic agent: "It may partly or ex-
clusively operate upon the experience of the man himself;
but, the more perfect the artist, the more completely
separate in him will be the man who suffers and mind
which creates; the more perfectly will the mind digest
and transmute the passions which are its material." [66]
Furthermore, it follows that elements which enter into
the creation of a work are in themselves rather diverse.
The intensity of the poetry is another thing again than
the intensity of the experience which one attributes to
the poet. Gourmont observed that the reader often "con-
fuses emotions with the expression of emotions," which is
indeed a different matter, because if the emotion is always true, the expression, by a man of genius or talent,
clothes it "in the character of art, artificial and voluntary."
Art requires "sang-froid," which it is the nature of the
emotions to make one lose. "When one is the prey of
the emotions, one's art loses its hold on them." [67]

The question of the role of personality in art was one
point of contention between Eliot and Gourmont; the
role of literary tradition was another. E. J. H. Greene, in
concluding his book *T. S. Eliot et la France*, states that
the influence of Gourmont on Eliot was "decisive" in all
matters of style. However, "in accepting, on the one hand,
Benda's analysis of the attitude of contemporary society
toward art and the artist, and in deepening, on the other
hand, thanks in part to Maurras' *L'Avenir de l'Intelligence*, the feeling for tradition implanted by Babbitt,
Eliot added to his critical ideas a dimension lacking in the
work of Gourmont." [68]

This charge—that Gourmont lacked feeling for tradition—is a familiar one, and one of which Gourmont
himself was only too aware. In an article written expressly
for publication in the United States,[69] he stated his position: "We must not make too much of tradition. It is no
great merit to place our feet exactly in the tracks which
the road indicates; it is a natural tendency. . . . the deed

is less meritorious than unavoidable." "Tradition," he continues, "is a great power opposing the originality of writers." Subjection to literary tradition can be very oppressive, a real yoke when the fashion is obedience to tradition; hence the literature of the eighteenth century and of the First Empire. One must distinguish, Gourmont explained, between "continuous" and "discontinuous" or "renewed" tradition. The seventeenth century and classic antiquity, Romanticism and the Middle Ages—these represent "renewed" tradition. Moreover, a tradition is most fertile, Gourmont affirmed, when the period or style being renewed is most distant and unknown.

So it is apparent that Gourmont, like all French writers, was much concerned with tradition and his relation to it. He admitted that he was, in a sense, traditional: "My tradition is not only French; it is European." He claimed that he was most impressed by the poetry of Shakespeare, Byron, and Dante. Goethe, he said, "enchanted my reason"; Schopenhauer "began my philosophical education"; Nietzsche gave a "principle for my repugnance to spiritualistic morality." He was much impressed by the satire of Swift and Cervantes, and the two books which he claimed "opened the world to my soul" were Stendhal's *De l'amour* and *Madame Bovary*.

In the same *Poetry* article Gourmont gave a candid appraisal of himself:

> I have often fought against my natural tendencies, often praised a state which was quite inaccessible to me; and several of my books are merely protests against myself.[70] For a long time I have had no aggressive opinions on anything, but, with the débris of my old convictions, deeper convictions have been formed in me with which I judge even those matters on which I am silent. . . .
>
> The true tradition of the French mind is the liberty of mind. To discuss all questions anew, to admit none save those which can be resolved *a priori*, only to admit the best reasons and to consider as the best those which contain a principle of independence. To remember that no tradition is worth the tradition of liberty. To be oneself, to disregard those who speak to one in the name of a

dogma; but not to be one's own dupe, and not to wish to impose on others that liberty of which the constitution of their brains renders them incapable. . . .

At bottom everything in literature is useless except literary pleasure, but literary pleasure depends upon the quality of sensibility. All discussions die against the wall of personal sensibility, which is flesh on the inside and on the outside is a wall of stone. There is a way to turn it about, but this you do not know.

Although Gourmont believed, like Eliot, that a writer, in attaching himself to a tradition, modifies that tradition, it is evident that he was greatly at odds with Eliot in other matters concerning a writer's relation to his predecessors. Both writers, in a sense, sought "liberation"—Gourmont from an overwhelming literary heritage, Eliot from the limitations of the individual ego. Reared in the classic French tradition, Gourmont needed to have the illusion of fleeing his heritage and being his own tradition. "The French tradition is so vast, so contradictory, that it lends itself to all tastes." However, he affirmed, French tradition is a terrible burden, a depressing list of imposing names from Emile Deschamps to Paul Verlaine. "It is a chaos, a bog in the forest. We can no longer see the sky. Cut them down! Cut them down!" Eliot, on the other hand, coming as he did after a period of vague sentimentalism and not having experienced the narrow tradition imposed by education in France, had soon perceived the need of establishing for himself a usable tradition.[71]

Gourmont, in his very struggles against tradition, remained squarely in the flow of the tradition. In his stubborn rejection of conventions and insistence on individual judgment as sole arbiter of literary merit, and in his belief in the importance of literature and intellectual activity in general and his great concern for the French language, Gourmont demonstrates the continuity of the French literary heritage and assures himself a position, however small, in its tradition.

Although Eliot found in the French writer what René Taupin describes as "free and lively thought, the sense of

fact; the living vision of those facts," he surpasses Gourmont in plenitude of conception. Gourmont said, "Every
word, every great style corresponds initially to a vision,"
but his conception of "vision" remained close to the
domain of the senses and of sensuality. Eliot took this idea
and expanded it: "The end of the enjoyment of poetry is a
pure contemplation from which all accidents of personal
emotion are removed . . . And without a labour which
is largely a labour of intelligence, we are unable to attain
that stage of vision *amor intellectualis Dei*." [72] Gourmont
thought that true books are those in which the author, in
discussing himself, recounts the manners, attitudes, and
emotions of his time; whereas Eliot granted the writer
only the right to arrange emotions and emotional experiences into larger structures. Eliot understood poetry
on a broader scale, as the living organization of experience
made at diverse periods and as "the living whole of all
the poetry that has ever been written." [73]

The period of Gourmont's direct influence on Eliot
probably ended with the 'twenties. From the time of the
publication of *For Launcelot Andrews* and *After Strange
Gods* up to the present moment, there has been a pro-
gressive divergence due in part to Eliot's movement towards absolutism and orthodoxy, and in part to the fact
that Eliot had, by 1927, drawn from Gourmont all that
was of use to him. In matters other than the "integrity of
art," the function of criticism, and the role of sensation
and sensibility in poetry, Eliot and Gourmont would
appear to be separated by a considerable abyss. In their
attitudes toward society, morality, sin, religion, and sex,
the two writers, save for a mutual taste for the aristocratic,
have nothing to say to one another. Even on the subject of
the sensibility, whose basic importance they both acknowledge, there would be slight rapport today, for in Eliot's
diagnosis of modern literature there has been the implicit
judgment that poetry is dying because of "liberal humanism." This liberal humanism is based on free or scientific
inquiry, which is in fundamental conflict with the philosophy of the Church. The cure for this condition, according

to Eliot, is orthodoxy, the submission to dogma and authoritative belief: artists should exemplify the "orthodox Christian sensibility." This attitude contains all that Gourmont detested. It is remarkable that two writers who held such widely differing opinions on other matters should have been so close in their theories on the writing of poetry.

vi

A considerable body of commentary has built up around the question of the extent of Imagism's debt to the French Symbolist movement. In an article in *La France* (May 5, 1915), Gourmont expressed his belief that the Symbolists were the immediate ancestors of the Imagist writers. In this article, which found great favor among the Anglo-American poets, Gourmont observed: "The English Imagists obviously derive from the French Symbolists. One sees this primarily in their horror of the cliché, their horror of the rhetorical and the grandiose, of the oratorical, a facile genre which the imitators of Victor Hugo have rendered permanently disgusting; the precision of language, clarity of vision, concentration of thought which they love to synthesize in a dominant image."

This passage was used by Amy Lowell to introduce an account of the Imagist movement in *Poetry* (VI, 1915); Aldington quoted it in the *Bruno Chap Book* (1915) and pronounced Swinburne, Tennyson, and Thompson to be English equivalents of the "disgusting" imitators of Hugo; and it appeared in the preface to *Some Imagist Poets* (1916) as part of the Imagist manifesto. This same preface also quotes a translation of Gourmont's definition of Symbolism (one of many he wrote) taken from his preface to the *Livres des Masques*: "Individualism in literature, liberty of art, abandonment of present forms . . . The sole excuse which a man can have for writing is to write down himself, to unveil for others the sort of world which mirrors itself in his individual glass . . . He should create his own aesthetic—and we should admit as many

aesthetics as there are original minds, and judge them for
what they are and not what they are not." To this the
author of the Imagist preface adds: "In this sense the
Imagists are descendents of the Symbolists; they are In-
dividualists."

The claims made by Gourmont and Imagists to a family
relationship between the Symbolists and the Anglo-
American movement are supported by two observers and
sharply questioned by a third. Taupin agrees with Gourmont's views of the Imagist heritage and adds that the
statements made on both sides show us "how perfect was
the community of thought on the art of writing between
the Imagists and de Gourmont." William Van O'Connor,
in a book published in 1948, sees no reason to revise Taupin's earlier judgment. O'Connor points out that it was
fundamentally from the *Problème du Style* that the important precepts for Imagist and Imagist-influenced poetry
came—"The idea that an analogy should be fused from
two different things seized upon by the imagination, and
that the style is primary, the subject secondary." [74]

Establishing a direct relationship between the writings
of Gourmont and the Imagists is one thing, but establishing a similar relationship between the Imagists and the
French Symbolists in general is another. Stanley Coffman
insists that the relation between the theory stated in the
1915–16 Imagist anthologies and the Symbolist aesthetic
is somewhat "ambiguous." He feels that the Imagists were
"obviously willing to permit belief in a fundamental
similarity between the two aesthetics." The similarity certainly does not entirely hold for Hulme or Pound, and
Coffman suspects that it was not really intended to hold
for the theory of the later group: "Association with Symbolism, a well established school, was to their advantage."
Pound, while concurring with Coffman's negative view of
the relationship between Symbolism and Imagism, was not
convinced of any "advantage" accruing to the latter:

> Imagism is not Symbolism. The Symbolists dealt in
> "association," that is, in a sort of allusion, almost of
> allegory. They degraded the symbol to the status of a

word. They made it a form of metonomy. One can be grossly "symbolic," for example, by using the word "cross" to mean "trial." The symbolists' *symbols* have a fixed value, like the numbers in arithmetic, like 1, 2, and 7. The imagists' images have a variable significance, like the signs a, b, and x in algebra.

Moreover, one does not want to be called a symbolist, because symbolism has usually been associated with mushy technique.[75]

Coffman sees the true relation between Imagism and Symbolism in this way: "The line of demarcation is clear: the poet could hold, with Hulme and the Imagists, that his art should be confined to the precise, external, physical world, or, with the early Symbolists, that it should attempt to penetrate the external to the vague and shadowy life beyond; he could deal strictly with man's sensitivity to and imaginative awareness of the external world, or he could use the external and man's consciousness as the basis for something beyond either." [76] In other words, one might say that a poet could "choose to derive" from either the Parnassian or the Symbolist aesthetic and choose either a Gautier or a Mallarmé as a forebear.

What especially complicates this discussion, and makes Pound's description of Symbolism seem perversely limited, is the fact that one must speak of Symbolist aesthetics in the plural. Although the French poets were united on most points, they differed on others and varied somewhat in their practice. They concurred, by and large, in what they abhorred in poetry, and it was this common denominator that Gourmont emphasized in the first part of the passage quoted from *La France*. He believed that Symbolists in general and Imagists were united in what they *opposed*. In the last part of the passage Gourmont is indeed describing Imagist doctrine rather than that of the early Symbolists; and in the quoted portion of the preface to *Livres des Masques*, Gourmont again strikes a common note, the call for individualism, freedom, and innovation in art, to which Symbolists and Imagists alike would strongly assert, whatever their other differences.

In matters of linguistic ideals the two movements were no doubt very close, but their theories, especially regarding the symbolic function of the natural world, are sharply at variance. The Imagists did not use symbols in the Symbolist sense; they were concerned with the precise rendering of the natural object, especially as that object appears to the eye. Generally speaking, in the Symbolist poem the image is partial: the contours of the evoked object are formed gradually by a succession of images, the synthesis being made by the reader. As Mallarmé said, much of the aesthetic pleasure gained by the reader comes from his active participation in creating the poem and in solving its mystery. For the Imagist, however, the image is the synthesis itself. The image, the new word, springs from the sensation which is its base—it *is* that sensation directly communicated.

Furthermore, for the Symbolist, the image is not an end but a departure. It tends to be dissipated in the process of suggesting the *Au-delà*, the spiritual or Platonic Beyond. For the Imagist, on the other hand, the image must remain clear and sharp, made for the eye. It must not be effaced, but must be admired in all its clarity, for it is the center of the poet's thought. Indeed, as Taupin points out, the difference between the "image" of the Imagist and "symbol" of the Symbolist is mainly a difference of precision. The Symbolist seeks to leave the image vague, to associate partial and multiple images in a manner as to render the emotion and its "harmonics." Furthermore, in the Symbolist world, which is a "forest of symbols," or as Northrop Frye puts it, "a shrine of mysterious oracles," perception, as direct vision, must be replaced by intuition. The referential role of words is subordinated to a pattern of metaphor, to the juxtaposing of images. The images do not state or point to anything outside the poem so much as they point to one another, thereby suggesting or evoking the mood which informs the poem. In such poetry the individual word does not echo the thing but other words, and the immediate impact the poem makes on the reader is that of incantation, a harmony of

sounds, and a sense of expanding imaginative richness
unlimited by either denotation or traditional connota-
tion. The "meaning" of such poetry resides not in the
visual sensation rendered intact, but in the sensuous and
suggestive qualities of the language itself. As Valéry says,
speaking of Mallarmé's work, the meaning in poetry consists in "the extension—at first empirical, then systematic
and pure—of certain properties of language." [77] Elsewhere
Valéry refers to Mallarmé's aim as "the desire to display,
to conserve through the thoughts, and to develop for their
own sakes, the forms of language." [78]

This is a view of poetry for which the later Gourmont—
the Gourmont the Imagists knew and admired—could
not have been the spokesman. In fact, William Van
O'Connor is probably right in stating that "the insistence
of Gourmont upon the exact word possibly helped cause
the second-generation Symbolists to move toward the
real rather than continue the Baudelairean tradition of
using symbols for their 'liberating value,' of probing subjective levels of consciousness and unconsciousness for
poetic material." [79] Also, it is evident that the Imagists
were as much in the line of the Parnassians as of the
Symbolists. They were the descendents of the latter movement mainly in the sense in which Gourmont had characterized that movement—the new and original expression
of individual feelings and perceptions; the quest for a
fresh language, devoid of rhetoric, cliché, and verbal
padding; and the insistence on absolute freedom from
moral, social, and religious concerns. In sum, it was their
emphasis on sensation that shows their affiliation with the
Gourmontian rather than the Mallarméan form of symbolism. The Imagists, like Gourmont, believed that style
is feeling, seeing, and thinking, and nothing more. Like
him, they thought that the concrete must be preferred to
the abstract; that an idea is an image, but worn and
weakened; that sensation is at the base of everything, of
intellectual as well as physical life.

There remains some question, nevertheless, as to
whether the Imagists succeeded in grasping the total

significance of Gourmont's theory of style. Gourmont demanded that a writer be capable of incorporating his entire sensibility into his language, including the emotions and the reason, which is only the "sensibility crystallized." The Imagists, however, were often inclined to reduce poetry to a simple vehicle of the sensations, or to a purely descriptive art, lacking the full-bodied quality Gourmont had in fact intended.

It is to be expected that the Imagists, like Gourmont's other followers, would pick and choose from his works, select and reject, ignore and perhaps distort—such is the nature of "influence." But Gourmont could not have hoped for greater success—for more faithful disciples, more eager borrowers, or, for that matter, more indignant disputers than those he had. For while he has faded somewhat from the position of high esteem which he occupied during and immediately following his lifetime, his works did inspire and guide an important group of young writers and are recognized by today's scholars as having contributed significantly to modern literature.

If any part of Gourmont's literature lives into the future it will probably not be his imaginative writing. His novels, plays, and perhaps his poetry seem destined to be read only by students seeking understanding of his work as a whole, for it is only in that light that they can command attention. His essays and critiques, on the other hand, deserve present and future readers, as they remain an excellent statement of a fundamental and perennial point of view. For the historically-minded, Gourmont reflects, perhaps better than any other writer, the cross-currents of literary opinion of his period, while at the same time he gives the impressionist position in criticism its most lucid and convincing exposition. His writings will appeal primarily to other writers and critics; he can never have a popular following. But in his chosen fields of study, and especially in his demonstration of the role of sensation and the sensibility in artistic creation and criticism, his work has a permanent value.

NOTES

MANY OF GOURMONT'S WORKS were published in series of volumes, namely the *Promenades philosophiques*, the *Promenades littéraires*, and the *Epilogues*. In the original they are designated as "première série," "deuxième série," etc. For simplicity's sake I refer to the different series merely by Roman numerals I, II, etc. Full titles of works are given in the first footnote entries; thereafter abbreviations are used: *Prom. phil.* I, *Epil.* IV, and so on. All works by Gourmont cited in this book were published in Paris by Mercure de France, unless otherwise indicated. Except when another translator is named, all translations are my own.

1—The Man

1. *The Tenth Muse*. New York, 1958, p. 266.

2. See James Laver, *The First Decadent: Being the Strange Life of J.-K. Huysmans*. London, 1954.

3. Paul Léautaud, *Journal littéraire*, vol. 1. Paris, 1955, pp. 347–48.

4. But Fleuret recalls Gourmont's difficulties in cafes, where waitresses did not like to wait on him, and where occasionally people would change tables to avoid having to look at him. Fleuret also recounts Apollinaire's story about Gourmont: he would walk at night, displaying a 100 franc note openly to the "filles" who, on closer look at him, would turn on their heels and flee. (Fernand Fleuret, *De Gilles de Rais à Guillaume Apollinaire*. Paris, 1933, pp. 213–14.)

5. Dr. Paul Voivenel, *Remy de Gourmont, vu par son médécin*. Paris: Edition du Siècle, n.d., p. 82.

6. Legrand-Chabrier, *Remy de Gourmont, son Oeuvre.* Paris, 1925, p. 37.

7. Jean de Gourmont assures us that Remy considered his position at the library "the most terrible of slaveries," so its loss could not have been an insupportable shock. (*Souvenirs sur Remy.* Paris, 1924, p. 32.)

8. *Promenades littéraires,* IV, 34–35. This occurred sometime during the late 1880's. Gourmont himself is vague about the date.

9. Laurence H. Bussard, "French Literary Criticism in the *Mercure de France,* 1890–1899." Unpublished doctoral dissertation, Univ. of Illinois, 1940, p. 85.

10. *De Mon Temps.* Paris, 1933 (4th ed.), p. 145.

11. *Prom. litt.* V, 154. Gourmont here seems willfully unaware of the poetry, at once symbolist and religious, of Claudel and Jammes.

12. Roger Shattuck describes Mme. de Courrière as "an aging, lecherous, ambitious woman, who chased priests." In 1896 "the old lady," as she was called, made advances to Gourmont's friend, Alfred Jarry, who apparently accepted her attentions for a while, for there resulted a painful rupture of relations between Gourmont and Jarry. See *The Banquet Years.* New York, 1961, p. 195.

13. See Mario Praz, *The Romantic Agony,* trans. Angus Davidson. London, 1951 (2nd ed.), pp. 351–52.

14. "Approaches to Remy de Gourmont," *Dial,* LXX (Feb. 1921), p. 134.

15. Garnet Rees, *Remy de Gourmont, essai de biographie intellectuelle.* Paris, 1940 (Doctoral dissertation, Sorbonne, 1939), p. 93.

2—Gourmont's Philosophy

1. *Le Chemin de Velours,* pp. 221–22.

2. "Literary Criticism in France, Part I," *Scrutiny,* Sept. 1939. Reprinted in *Critiques and Essays in Criticism,* R. W. Stallman, ed. New York, 1949, p. 425.

3. A. G. Lehmann, *The Symbolist Aesthetic in France, 1885–1895.* Oxford, 1950, p. 38.

4. *Ibid.,* p. 43.

5. A perennial problem. Henri Peyre has shown that most all great writers of all periods were to some extent condemned as "obscure" by able critics and writers of their own time. Peyre, in his *Writers and Their Critics,* cites Gourmont approvingly on the regrettable lack of an enriching obscurity in French literature.

6. Northrop Frye, "Yeats and the Language of Symbolism," *Univ. of Toronto Quarterly,* XVII (Oct. 1947), 8.

7. Laurence H. Bussard, "French Literary Criticism in the *Mercure de France,* 1890–1899," pp. 85–88.

8. *Mercure de France,* I, 333.

9. See Brunetière's two articles in the *Revue des Deux Mondes:* "Symbolisme et décadens [sic]," XC, sér. 3 (Nov.–Dec. 1888), 217; and "Le Symbolisme contemporain," CIV, sér. 3 (Mar.–Apr. 1891), 688.

10. *La Vie littéraire,* vol. III. Paris (4 vols. 1889–95), pp. 233–35. I am indebted to Bussard's dissertation for many of these references.

11. *Ibid.,* I, 299.

12. *Ibid.,* II, 200.

13. *Ibid.,* IV, 104.

14. *Ibid.,* IV, 209.

15. Burton Rascoe, *Titans of Literature.* New York, 1932, pp. 445, 430–31.

16. *Les Contemporaines,* III (1898–1918). Paris, 1918, p. 239.

17. *Ibid.,* IV, 65.

18. *Ibid.,* IV, 70–71.

19. *Témoignages,* 2me série. Paris, 1911, p. 154.

20. *Sixtine,* p. 27.

21. *Prom. phil.* I, 79–105.

22. Lehmann, *Symbolist Aesthetic,* p. 44.

23. *Prom. phil.* I, 105.

24. *Ibid.,* 133.

25. *Prom. phil.* V, 154.

26. Eugène Bencze, *La Doctrine esthétique de Remy de Gourmont*. Toulouse, 1928, p. 58.

27. *Epilogues* II, 65.

28. *Prom. phil.* II, 294–95.

29. *Epil.* IV, 267; *Prom. phil.* III, 219.

30. *Epil.* III, 223.

31. *Chemin de Velours*, 87–89.

32. *Epil.* II, 130.

33. *Mercure de France*, III (1906), 247.

34. *Prom. phil.* II, 148–49.

35. *Physique de l'Amour, Essai sur l'instinct sexuel.* Paris, 1944 ed., pp. 10–11.

36. Garnet Rees, *Remy de Gourmont*, pp. 174–75.

37. *From Rousseau to Proust.* London, 1936, pp. 311, 315.

38. *Culture des Idées*, pp. 43–44.

39. Mallarmé, *Oeuvres complètes*, Pléiade ed. Paris, 1945, p. 857.

40. *Culture des Idées*, p. 45.

41. For example, A. G. Lehman, *Symbolist Aesthetic*, pp. 120–21. Also see R. G. Collingwood, *The Principles of Art.* Oxford, The Clarendon Press, 1938, p. 281.

42. *Culture des Idées*, p. 44.

43. Bencze, *Doctrine esthétique de Remy de Gourmont*, p. 69.

44. *Prom. phil.* I, 128. J. W. Krutch sees Gourmont's dilemma as an unsavory fruit of his "nihilism," *Nation*, vol. 127 (Oct. 10, 1928), p. 358. Kenneth Burke believes Gourmont's situation is not a dilemma, but a "healthy equipollence of material basis and spiritual fulfillment." "Approaches to Remy de Gourmont," *Dial*, LXX (Feb. 1921), 130. Reprinted in *Counterstatement* as part of "Three Adepts of Pure Literature." Los Altos, Calif., 1953.

45. *Lettres à l'Amazone*, p. 223.

46. Rees, *Remy de Gourmont*, pp. 145–46.

47. *Prom. phil.* I, 9.

48. *Epil.* III, 174.

49. *Prom. litt.* I, 13.

50. *Prom. litt.* I, 96–98.

51. *Une Nuit au Luxembourg*, p. 173.

52. *Epil.* II, 64–65.

53. *Le Problème du Style*, p. 8.

54. *Prom. phil.* I, 130.

55. *Epil.* III, 68.

56. Paul Escoube, *Remy de Gourmont et son Oeuvre.* Paris, 1921, p. 56.

57. The first two essays appear in *La Culture des Idées* and the second two in *Le Chemin de Velours*. All four have been translated into English by William Aspenwall Bradley in a volume entitled *Decadence and Other Essays in the Culture of Ideas*, New York, 1921.

58. *Culture des Idées*, p. 69.

59. *Ibid.*, p. 73.

60. *Ibid.*, pp. 74–75.

61. Cf. Henri Peyre: "There is only one type of decadence which is dangerous in art and literature, and unfortunately critics seldom scourge it as it deserves: it consists in being conventional and imitative, in tritely expressing cheap and superficial emotions." *Writers and Their Critics*, Ithaca, N. Y., 1944, p. 181.

62. "De Gourmont on 'Dissociation,'" *A Rhetoric of Motives.* New York, 1950, pp. 150–51.

63. Krutch, *Nation*, vol. 127, pp. 357–58.

64. *A Rhetoric of Motives*, p. 153.

65. *Counterstatement.* Los Altos, Calif., 1953, p. 24.

66. *La Culture des Idées*, p. 97.

67. Brunet, *Ombres vivantes.* Paris, 1936, p. 311.

68. *Journal litt.* I, 116–20.

69. "Remy de Gourmont critique," *PMLA*, LII, no. 4 (Dec. 1937), 1152.

3—Gourmont's Literary Criticism

1. For much information on the early years of the *Mercure de France*, I am indebted to Laurence H. Bussard, "French Literary Criticism in the *Mercure de*

France, 1890–1899." Unpub. doct. diss., Univ. of Illinois, 1940.

2. *Revue Encyclopédique,* December, 1896.

3. "De la critique," *Mercure de France,* Feb. 1897, p. 408.

4. *Deuxième Livre des Masques,* preface (1898).

5. In *Chemin de Velours,* pp. 226–31.

6. *Ibid.,* pp. 129–62.

7. Bencze, *Doctrine esthétique de Remy de Gourmont,* p. 107. I am much indebted in this section to Bencze's perceptive study.

8. Both Gourmont and Sainte-Beuve spoke of "the general sensibility of an era," and T. S. Eliot often echoes this concept.

9. *Prom. phil.* I, 33–44.

10. *Ibid.,* 35. Cf. T. S. Eliot: "In our time, the most vigorous creative minds are philosophic minds, are, in short, creative of values." *Criterion,* Oct. 1927, p. 751.

11. *Prom. phil.,* I, 43. For a critique of Gourmont's views on Sainte-Beuve, see Martin Turnell, "Literary Criticism in France," in R. W. Stallman (ed.), *Critiques and Essays in Criticism.* New York, 1949, p. 430. (Reprinted from *Scrutiny,* Sept. and Dec. 1939, pp. 421–34.) Also see Henri Peyre, *Writers and Their Critics,* pp. 121–22. Peyre points out that "minor" critics like Baudelaire and Gourmont were usually far better judges of contemporary writers than were such major critics as Taine, Sainte-Beuve, and Faguet.

12. *Essais sur la littérature contemporaine.* Paris, 1896 (3rd ed.), pp. 1–30.

13. *Les Contemporains.* Paris, 1898–1918. Quotes from vol. I, page v, and vol. II, p. vi.

14. *Ibid.,* I, 247.

15. *Livre des Masques,* I, Preface, 13.

16. *Prom. litt.* I, 13.

17. *Ibid.,* 13–14. "Subject" is not important, but "thought," which is another matter, is all-important. This distinction is further developed in a later chapter.

18. In Stallman, *Critiques and Essays,* p. 441.

19. Lemaître, *Les Contemporains,* III, 342.

20. *Prom. litt.* I, 96–104.

21. Peyre, "The Criticism of Contemporary Writing," *Lectures in Criticism.* New York, 1949, p. 143.

22. Unpublished doctoral dissertation, New York University, 1942.

23. "Two French Critics, Emile Faguet and Remy de Gourmont," in *Aspects and Impressions.* New York, 1922, pp. 217–18.

24. *Remy de Gourmont, essai de Biographie intellectuelle,* p. 120.

25. *Epil.* III, 19–20.

26. *Prom. litt.* IV, 82.

27. One is reminded of Henry Sidgwick's question: How is one to distinguish those contradictions which may be taken as evidence of error from those other contradictions that are a token of a higher truth?

28. Turnell, in Stallman, *Critiques and Essays;* Warren Ramsay in his *Jules Laforgue and the Ironic Inheritance;* and Guy Michaud in his *Message poétique du Symbolisme.*

29. In Stallman, *Critiques and Essays,* p. 61.

4—The Problem of Style

1. For example, Irving Babbitt in his *Masters of French Criticism* and Kenneth Burke in *Counter-Statement.* Burke later rounds out his view of Gourmont in his study of the "Dissociation of Ideas" in A *Rhetoric of Motives.*

2. "L'Ivresse verbale," *Chemin de Velours,* pp. 240–41.

3. *Esthétique de la Langue française,* Preface, 7.

4. *Ibid.,* p. 8.

5. *L'Art d'écrire enseigné en vingt leçons.* This work is still in print and can be seen on display in bookstores around the Sorbonne. Gourmont's *Le Problème du Style* is long out of print and very difficult to find. Albalat seems to have survived his refutation.

6. *Le Problème du Style,* pp. 9, 19, 32.

7. *Ibid.,* 104.

8. 'Du Style ou de l'Ecriture," *La Culture des Idées,* p. 17.

9. *Le problème du Style,* p. 53.

10. *Ibid.,* pp. 34–35.

11. *Ibid.,* pp. 45–46. This might well apply to some of Gourmont's own early writing, his dramas especially, where he is consciously demonstrating a philosophical thesis.

12. *Ibid.,* p. 50.

13. *Ibid.,* p. 81.

14. *Ibid.,* pp. 67–70.

15. *Ibid.,* pp. 70–71.

16. *Ibid.,* p. 80.

17. *Ibid.,* p. 73.

18. *Ibid.,* p. 81. For an interesting discussion of Gourmont's study of Taine's style, see Albert Thibaudet, "La Critique et le Style," *Reflexions sur la Critique.* Paris, 1939, pp. 58–71.

19. *Prob. du Style,* p. 153.

20. *Cult. des Idées,* p. 9. Here Gourmont is directly quoting Buffon.

21. *Ibid.,* pp. 10–11.

22. *Prom. litt.* I, 17.

23. *Ibid.,* p. 66.

24. *Prom. phil.* I, 233.

25. *Cult. des Idées,* p. 17.

26. *English Literature and Ideas in the Twentieth Century.* London, 1946, p. 169.

27. *Prob. du Style,* pp. 89–90.

28. *Ibid.,* p. 46.

29. *Ibid.,* p. 93.

30. *Ibid.,* p. 51. One of Gourmont's limitations was his inability to accept the greatness of the French neoclassical writers. One would expect that Racine's concern for sexual passion would have interested Gourmont, but such was not the case.

31. Murry, *The Problem of Style.* London, 1925, p. 14.

32. Suckling, *Paul Valéry and the Civilized Mind.* London, 1955, pp. 39–41.

33. *Ibid.*, p. 81.

34. *Prob. du Style*, pp. 104–5.

35. Thibaudet, "La Critique et le Style," *Reflexions,* pp. 68–70.

36. See especially Miss Langer's discussion of "The Comic Rhythm" in *Feeling and Form.* New York, 1953. In her analysis of comedy Miss Langer emphasizes the efforts of living things "to persist in a particular chemical balance, to maintain a particular temperature, to repeat particular functions, and to develop along particular lines, achieving a growth that seems to be preformed in their earliest rudimentary, protoplasmic structure"—which is strongly reminiscent of Gourmont's physiologically based theories. When Miss Langer states that comic action is the struggle of the human organism to regain "its rhythm of animal existence," to overcome obstacles to "the round of conditioned and conditioning organic processes that produces the life rhythm," she is very close to Gourmont both in his science-oriented theories in general and his belief, adapted from the biologist Quinton, that all life strives to maintain the conditions of its origins.

5—Gourmont and the Anglo-Americans

1. In a letter from Huneker to W. C. Brownell, January 29, 1910: "There are a hundred books called *Impressions* and only two called *Promenades,* Stendhal's and de Gourmont's. Hence my *Promenades of an Impressionist.*"

2. "The Example of Remy de Gourmont," *Criterion,* X (July 1931), 614–25. Thompson does acknowledge Gourmont, among others, in his Preface.

3. *Forty Immortals.* New York, 1926, pp. 18–28.

4. *The Critical Game.* New York, 1922, p. 159.

5. See Deryk Mossop, "Un Disciple de Gourmont: Richard Aldington," *Revue de Littérature Comparée,* XXV (1951), 403–35.

6. See Bibliography for contents of this issue.

7. For a complete listing of translations of Gourmont's works, see Bibliography.

8. L. C. Bruenig, "F. S. Flint, Imagism's Maître d'Ecole," *Comparative Literature*, IV, no. 2 (Spring 1952), 118–36.

9. *Prob. du Style*, p. 171.

10. Ezra Pound sharply questions the role and influence of Hulme. See his "This Hulme Business," *The Townsman*, Jan. 1938. Reprinted in an appendix to Hugh Kenner's *The Poetry of Ezra Pound*. New York and London, 1951.

11. "The Example of Remy de Gourmont," 619–20.

12. William Van O'Connor, *Sense and Sensibility in Modern Poetry*. Chicago, 1948, p. 67.

13. Aldington, "Modern Poetry and the Imagists," *Poetry*, June 5, 1914.

14. When Elinor Wylie wrote to Amy Lowell to express her appreciation of *Six French Poets*, she said, " 'Velvet Shoes' would never have been written but for the Simone poems of de Gourmont—he made me think of stepping softly, like that, without emotion." Cited by S. Foster Damon, *Amy Lowell, A Chronicle*. Boston, 1935, pp. 594–95.

15. *Prob. du Style*, p. 9.

16. *Speculations*. London, 1924, p. 242.

17. *Prob. du Style*, pp. 36–37.

18. *Speculations*, p. 152.

19. *Ibid.*, pp. 163–64.

20. From "Romanticism and Classicism," *Ibid.*, pp. 134–35.

21. From "Bergson's Theory of Art," *Ibid.*, p. 151.

22. In *A Lecture on Modern Poetry*, quoted by Mossop, p. 44.

23. For much of this information about Richard Aldington and Amy Lowell, I am indebted to S. Foster Damon's *Amy Lowell, A Chronicle*, pp. 275–89.

24. *Poetry*, Jan. 1916, p. 120.

25. *Imagism, A Chapter for the History of Modern Poetry*. Norman, Oklahoma, 1951, pp. 88–89.

26. *The Letters of Ezra Pound, 1907–1941*. Edited by D. D. Paige. New York, 1950, pp. 217–18. A translation of Pound's French would be somewhat as follows:

"You have in *Poetry*, Chicago (1912, I believe), my first quoting of French contemporaries. Time of the unanimists. In all modesty, I believe that I was oriented before knowing the modern French poets. That I profited from their technical inventions (as Edison or any other man of science profits from discoveries). There are, also, the ancients: Villon, The Troubadors.

"You will find in my *The Spirit of Romance*, published in 1910, what I knew—before approaching the modern French . . .

"Another dissociation to make: sometimes one learns, or is subject to the 'influence' of an idea—sometimes in a struggle against barbarism, one seeks a support—one arms himself with the prestige of a civilized and recognized man in order to combat American imbecility.

"I have cited Gourmont, and I have just given a new version of *Ta Hio* of Confucius, because I find there formulations of ideas which seem to me useful in civilizing America (tentative). [Pound might have meant the feminine *tentative*, meaning an "effort" or "attempt."] I revere good sense rather than originality (whether of Remy de Gourmont, whether of Confucius)." And the next line of Pound's French:

"Symbol?? I have never read 'the ideas of symbolists' on that subject. . . . I do not recall anything of Gourmont's on the subject of 'symbol.' " Which seems a remarkable oversight, or lapse of memory, on Pound's part.

27. "The Example of Remy de Gourmont," p. 617.

28. *Instigations*, pp. 35–36.

29. *Literary Essays of Ezra Pound*. Norfolk, Conn., 1954, p. 343. René Taupin thinks that Amy Lowell's *Lilacs* and John Gould Fletcher's *In the City of Night* are indebted to the *Litanies*. Regarding e. e. cummings' *Sunset* (". . . chants the litanies the great bells are ringing with rose"), Laura Riding and Robert Graves observe: "The title might undergo some amplification because of a veiled literary reference in lines five and six [above] to Remy de Gourmont's *Litanies de la Rose*: it might reasonably include some acknowledgement of the poet's debt to

French influence, and read 'Sunset Piece: After Reading Remy de Gourmont.'" (A *Survey of Modernist Poetry*. New York, 1928, pp. 13–14.) William York Tindall believes that T. S. Eliot "imitated" the *Litanies* in the second part of *Ash Wednesday* (*Forces in Modern British Literature*, New York, 1956, p. 281). John J. Espey has pointed out some "haunting" echoes of Gourmont in Eliot's work, such as "the possible relation between . . . the je verai dans/L'eau clair son pied nu' of *Divertissements* (p. 99) and 'through the water pale and thin/ Still shine the unoffending feet' of 'Mr. Eliot's Sunday Morning Service' or even the negative echo of something like 'Avril est revenu pour jouer avec nous' (*Divertissements*, p. 89) in the opening of *The Waste Land*, though in the latter instance one can, of course, point to all kinds of things." From a personal letter to the author, August 30, 1962.

30. *Gaudier-Brzeska, a Memoire*. London and New York, 1916, p. 97.

31. Kenner, *The Poetry of Ezra Pound*. New York and London, 1951, pp. 114–15.

32. *Ezra Pound's Mauberley: a Study in Composition*. Berkeley, 1955, p. 67.

33. *Ibid.*, p. 75.

34. *Ibid.*, p. 82.

35. *Pavannes and Divisions*. New York, 1918, p. 97.

36. From letters dated "September?, 1915" and January, 1915, in Paige, *Letters of Ezra Pound*.

37. For a study of Eliot's relations with various French writers, see E. J. H. Greene's *T. S. Eliot et la France*. Paris, 1951.

38. *Problème du Style*, pp. 107, 81. Gourmont also advances this theory in two earlier essays in *La Culture des Idées*: "La Dernière Conséquence de l'Idéalisme" and "La Création subconsciente."

39. *The Sacred Wood*. London, 1928, p. 14.

40. *Egoist*, Oct. 1918, p. 114.

41. *Sacred Wood*, pp. 128–36.

42. The phrase which Eliot omits is Gourmont's defini-

tion of sensibility: "And by sensibility I mean, here as elsewhere, the general power of feeling as it is unequally developed in each human being. The sensibility includes the reason itself, which is only the sensibility crystallized." (*Problème du Style*, p. 107.) Eliot always leaves Gourmont's words in the original French, which I have here, and elsewhere, translated.

43. *Sacred Wood*, pp. 139–40.

44. *Selected Essays*, 1917–32. New York, 1932, p. 246.

45. *Ibid.*, p. 249.

46. *Prom. litt.* I (1904), 105–6, 110.

47. See F. W. Bateson "Contribution to a Dictionary of Critical Terms: 'Dissociation of Sensibility,'" *Essays in Criticism*, I, no. 3, p. 303. This idea was also suggested by René Taupin, *L'Influence du Symbolisme français sur la Poésie américaine* (de 1910 à 1920). Paris, 1929; and by J. D. R. Mossop, "Remy de Gourmont en Angleterre." Unpub. doctoral dissertation, Sorbonne, 1929.

48. *Selected Essays*, p. 247.

49. Bateson, p. 308. Eric Thompson, in a reply to Bateson, sees the philosophy of F. H. Bradley, about whom Eliot had written an unpublished doctoral thesis while at Harvard, as the source of Eliot's conception of the dissociation of sensibility. Bateson's answer indicated that he remained unconvinced. But it seems quite probable that more than one source could be involved. *Essays in Criticism*, II, No. 2, pp. 207–14.

50. T. S. Apteryx (one of Eliot's early pseudonyms), *Egoist*, May 1918, p. 70.

51. *Sacred Wood*, p. 58. Eliot uses the term "unconscious" and Gourmont uses "subconscious," but we are here considering the two expressions as referring to essentially the same concept.

52. *Ibid.*, 136. Eliot quotes Maurras' words in the original French.

53. *Prob. du Style*, p. 107.

54. *Sacred Wood*, p. 15.

55. *Egoist*, Oct. 1918, p. 113.

56. *Sacred Wood*, p. 11.

57. *Prob. du Style*, p. 60.

58. *Sacred Wood*, pp. 8–12. On this important point the influence of Benda is added to that of Gourmont. See *Belphégor*, pp. 34–35, cited by Greene, *Eliot et la France*, p. 152.

59. *Prob. du Style*, p. 40.

60. *Sacred Wood*, pp. 54–56.

61. *Le Chemin de Velours* (1902), pp. 154–58. Eliot's version is: "A common inheritance and a common cause unite artists consciously or unconsciously: it must be admitted that the union is mostly unconscious. Between the true artists of any time there is, I believe, an unconscious community." *Selected Essays*, p. 13.

62. *Sacred Wood*, pp. 50–51.

63. *Ibid.*, p. 112.

64. *Prom. litt.* IV, 191.

65. *Sacred Wood*, pp. 57–58.

66. *Ibid.*, pp. 56, 54. E. J. H. Greene points out that Eliot, in elaborating this theory, was building on Gourmont's "La Création subconsciente" in *La Culture des Idées*.

67. *Prom. phil.* IV, 221.

68. *T. S. Eliot et la France*, p. 209. My translation from Mr. Greene's French.

69. "A French Poet on Tradition," *Poetry*, July 1914, pp. 154–60. Translated by Richard Aldington.

70. An example would be *Sixtine*, which is a criticism as well as an apology for extreme idealism and negation of action.

71. Taupin, *L'Influence*, pp. 214–15.

72. *Sacred Wood*, pp. 14–15.

73. *Ibid.*, p. 48.

74. O'Connor, *Sense and Sensibility in Modern Poetry*, p. 67.

75. *Gaudier-Brzeska, a Memoire*, p. 97.

76. Coffman, *Imagism*, 90.

77. Letter of Valéry, quoted by Albert Thibaudet, in *La Poésie de Stéphane Mallarmé*. Paris, 1926, pp. 376–77.

78. "Lettre Sur Mallarmé," *Variété II*. Paris, 1930, p. 189.

79. O'Connor, *Sense and Sensibility*, p. 70.

PRIMARY WORKS

A chronological list of Gourmont's works (omitting his works of "vulgarization," 1882–83), original editions, all published in Paris and all by Mercure de France unless otherwise stated. If an edition other than the original was used, it is indicated in parentheses.

Novels, Stories, Poetry, and Drama

1886 *Merlette*, novel. Plon, Nourrit, et Cie., 287 pp.
1890 *Sixtine, roman de la vie cérébrale*. Savine, 314 pp.
      Mercure de France, 1923 (13th ed.), 311 pp.
1892 *Lilith*, drama. Essais de l'art libre, 103 pp.
1892 *Litanies de la Rose*, poetry, 29 pp.
1893 *Théodat*, drama, 53 pp.
1893 *Le Fantôme*, story, 117 pp.
1893 *Fleurs de Jadis*, poetry, 21 pp.
1894 *Histoires magiques*, stories, 119 pp.
1894 *Le Château singulier*, story, 81 pp.
1894 *Proses moroses*, stories, 104 pp.
1894 *Hiéroglyphes*, poetry, 28 pp.
1894 (ed.) *L'Ymagier* (1894–96), recueil de gravures anciennes et nouvelles, d'études artistiques et philologiques, 64 pp.
1894 *Histoire tragique de la Princesse Phénissa*, story, 44 pp.
1895 *Phocas*, story, 29 pp.
1896 *Aucassin et Nicolette*, texte modernisé, 31 pp.
1896 *Pèlerin du Silence*, story, 23 pp.
1896 *Le Miracle de Théophile de Rutebeuf*, texte

modernisé avec une préface par Remy de Gourmont, 30 pp.

1897   *Le Vieux Roi*, tragédie nouvelle, drama, 57 pp.

1897   *Les Chevaux de Diomède*, novel, 254 pp.

1897   *Almanach de l'Ymagier*, zodiacal, astrologique,
littéraire, et prophétique. L'Ymagier (not in
Bibliothèque Nationale, British Museum, or
Library of Congress).

1898   *D'Un Pays lointain*, stories, 282 pp.

1899   *Les Saintes du Paradis*, poetry, 21 pp.

1899   *Le Songe d'une Femme*, *roman familier*, 250 pp.

1900   *Oraisons mauvaises*, poetry, 20 pp.

1901   *Simone, poème champêtre*, 53 pp.

1906   *Une Nuit au Luxembourg*, novel, 207 pp.

1907   *Un Coeur virginal*, novel, 250 pp.

1908   *Couleurs*, stories, 245 pp.

1910   *La Gloire de Don Ramire*, par Enrique Larreta.
Roman traduit de l'espagnol par Remy de
Gourmont.

1912   *Divertissements*, poetry. Crès, 177 pp.

1924   *L'Ombre d'une Femme*, pièce en un acte et en
prose et inédite. Champion.

1924   *Fin de Promenade et trois autre contes*. La Porte
Etroite, 53 pp.

Critical and philosophical essays; personal letters

1892   *Le Latin mystique*. Les Poètes de l'Antiphonaire
et la Symbolique au Moyen Age. Préface de
J.-K. Huysmans, xvi and 378 pp.

1893   *L'Idéalisme*, 60 pp. (Reprinted in *Le Chemin de
Velours*, 1902.)

1896   *La Poésie populaire*, 21 pp.

1896   *Le Livre des Masques* (6th ed., 1911), 270 pp.

1898   *Le Deuxième Livre des Masques*, 302 pp.

1899   *Esthétique de la Langue française*, 223 pp. (17th
ed., 1938, 343 pp.)

1900   *Les Petites Revues*, Essai de Bibliographie avec
préface de Remy de Gourmont, 34 pp.

1900   *La Culture des Idées*, 318 pp. (Nouvelle éd.,
        1910, 310 pp.)

1902   *Le Chemin de Velours*, 307 pp. (14th ed., 1924,
        321 pp.)

1902   *Le Problème du Style*, 282 pp.

1903   *Epilogues. Reflexions sur la vie* (1895–98), 337
        pp.

1903   *Physique de l'Amour, essai sur l'instinct sexuel*,
        295 pp. (47th ed., 1944, 201 pp.)

1904   *Judith Gautier*, biographie. Sansot, 34 pp.

1904   *Epilogues*, 2me série (1899–1901), 341 pp.

1904   *Promenades littéraires*, 1re série, 384 pp.

1905   *Promenades philosophiques*, 1re série, 344 pp.

1905   *Epilogues*, 3me série (1902–4), 360 pp.

1906   *Promenades littéraires*, 2me série, 346 pp.

1907   *Chronique stendhalienne*, par M. Coffe (pseud.).
        Chez Coffe et Cie., Editeurs Stendhaliens,
        Milan.

1907   *Dialogues des Amateurs* (*Epilogues*, 4me série,
        1905–7), 358 pp.

1908   *Dante, Béatrice, et la Poésie amoureuse*, 79 pp.

1908   *Promenades philosophiques*, 2me série, 300 pp.

1909   *Promenades littéraires*, 3me série, 432 pp.

1909   *Promenades philosophiques*, 3me série, 290 pp.

1910   *Nouveaux Dialogues des Amateurs* (*Epilogues*,
        5me série, 1907–10), 394 pp.

1912   *Promenades littéraires*, 4me série, 348 pp.

1912   *Le Chat de Misère, idées et images*. Messein, 120
        pp.

1912   *Je sors d'un bal paré*. Les Amis d'Edouard, pri-
        vately printed, limited edition, 72 pp.

1913   *Promenades littéraires*, 5me série, 288 pp.

1913   *Lettres d'un Satyre*. Crès, 189 pp.

1913   *La Petite Ville*, paysages, 126 pp.

1913   *Epilogues*, volume complémentaire (1905–12),
        338 pp.

1914   *Lettres à L'Amazone*. Crès, 361 pp. (Merc. de
        France, 1929, 284 pp.)

1915   *La Belgique littéraire*. Crès, 133 pp.

1915 *Pendant l'Orage.* Champion, 129 pp.

1916 *Dans la Tourmente.* Crès, 129 pp.

1916 *Pendant la Guerre,* Lettres pour l'Argentine, 268 pp.

1918 *Les Idées du Jour.* Crès, 2 volumes.

1918 *Monsieur Croquant.* Crès, 114 pp.

1919 *Trois légendes du Moyen Age.* Messein, 122 pp.

1919 *Les Pas sur le Sable, pensées.* Société littéraire de France, 63 pp.

1920 *Huit aphorismes.* Au Logis du Pan qui grimpe, Coutances.

1920 *Le Livret de l'Imagier.* Preface par G. A. Aurier. Editions du Sagittaire, 49 pp.

1920 *Pensées inédits.* Préface par G. Apollinaire. Editions de la Sirène.

1920 *La Patience de Grisélidis.* Editions du Sagittaire.

1921 *Lettres à Sixtine,* 203 pp.

1921 *Petits Crayons.* Crès, 199 pp.

1922 *Le Puits de la Verité.* Messein.

1922 *Extraits des Caractères de La Bruyère avec des Commentaires par Remy de Gourmont.* Imprimerie gourmontienne.

1922 *Pages choisies de Remy de Gourmont.* Edited, with preface, by Marcel Coulon, 434 pp.

1923 *Le Vase magique.* Les Quatorze, No. I, Le Divan, 118 pp.

1923 *Journal intime et inédit de feu Remy de Gourmont (1874–1880) recueilli par son frère.* Bernouard.

1924 *Dernières Pensées inédites.* Champion, 67 pp.

1925 *Nouvelles Dissociations.* Editions du Siècle, 192 pp.

1925 *Les Femmes et le Langage.* Chez Mme. Lesage, 49 pp.

1925 *La Fin de l'Art.* Cahiers de Paris, 127 pp.

1925 *Deux Poètes de la Nature: Bryant et Emerson.* La Centaine, 69 pp.

1926 *Lettres intimes à l'Amazone.* La Centaine, 305 pp.

1926 *Promenades littéraires,* 6me série, 240 pp.

172   BIBLIOGRAPHY

1926   *Le Joujou et Trois Autres Essais.* La Belle Page,
         52 pp.

1927   *Promenades littéraires,* 7me série, 254 pp.

1927   *Le Joujou patriotisme et documents annexés.* La
         Belle Page, 79 pp.

         Gourmont's works translated into English

1912   A *Night in the Luxembourg by Remy de Gour-
         mont,* trans. by Arthur Ransome, with a pref-
         ace and appendix. London: S. Swift, 1912; New
         York: Modern Library, 1926.

1916   *Théodat, the Old King,* trans. by Richard Alding-
         ton, in *Drama.* Washington, May 1916.

1919   Selections from Introduction to *Livres des
         Masques* and *Problème du Style,* in A *Modern
         Book of Criticism,* edited by Ludwig Lewisohn.
         New York: Modern Library, 1919.

1920   *Philosophic Nights in Paris,* being selections from
         the *Promenades philosophiques,* trans. by Isaac
         Goldberg. Boston: J. W. Luce, 1920, 190 pp.

1920–21 *Remy de Gourmont: Dust for Sparrows,*
         poems trans. by Ezra Pound. *The Dial,* nine
         numbers, September 1920 to May 1921.

1921   A *Virgin Heart, a novel by Remy de Gourmont,*
         authorized trans. by Aldous Huxley. New York:
         N. L. Brown, 1921; London: Brentano, 1922—
         Allen & Unwin, 1926; New York: Modern
         Library, 1927.

1921   *Decadence and other Essays on the Culture of
         Ideas by Remy de Gourmont,* authorized trans.
         by William Aspenwall Bradley. New York: Har-
         court, Brace Co., 1921. An essay from this book,
         "Of Style or Writing," is reprinted in *Essays
         in Modern Literary Criticism,* Ray B. West
         (ed.). New York: Rinehart, 1952.

1922   *Mr. Antiphilos, Satyr, by Remy de Gourmont,*
         trans. by John Howard with an introduction by
         Jack Lewis. New York: Lieber & Lewis, 1922.

1922   *Very Woman (Sixtine), a cerebral novel by* Remy de Gourmont, trans. by J. L. Barrets. New York: N. L. Brown, 1922.

1923   *The Horses of Diomedes,* trans. by C. Satoris in *New Freewoman,* August–December 1913, nine numbers; in *The Egoist,* January–March, four numbers; reprinted Boston: J. W. Luce, 1920, 249 pp.

1923   *Epigrams of Remy de Gourmont,* selected by Isaac Goldberg. Girard, Kansas: The Haldeman-Julius Co., 1923.

1924   *Stories in green, zinzolin, rose, purple, mauve, blue, and orange, by Remy de Gourmont,* trans. by Isaac Goldberg. Girard, Kansas: The Haldeman-Julius Co., 1924.

1924   *Stories in yellow, black, white, blue, violet and red, by Remy de Gourmont,* trans. by Isaac Goldberg. Girard, Kansas: The Haldeman-Julius Co., 1924.

1926   *Remy de Gourmont: The Natural Philosophy of Love,* trans. with a postscript by Ezra Pound. New York: Willey Book Co., 1940. For separate publication of postscript, see "Articles" below.

1927   *The Dream of a Woman,* trans. by Lewis Galantière. New York: Boni & Liveright, 1927.

1928   *Remy de Gourmont: Selections from all his Works,* chosen and trans. by Richard Aldington, with introduction, illustrated, with photographs, drawings, and woodcuts by André Rouveyre. Chicago: P. Covici, 1928, 2 vols. Abridged edition, 1 vol., London: Chatto and Windus, 1932.

1929   *Colours: faithfully rendered from the French of Remy de Gourmont,* trans. by Frederic Reeves Ashfield; with two supplementary colours by the translator. New York: Blue Fawn Publishers, 1929.

1931   *Letters to the Amazon, by Remy de Gourmont,* trans. with an introduction by Richard Aldington. London: Chatto and Windus, 1931.

1945   *Lilith, a play*, trans. by J. Heard in *Poet Lore*
[Boston], vol. 51 (1945), no. 4.

SELECTED SECONDARY WORKS

Books

Aldington, Richard. "Remy de Gourmont," *Literary Studies and Reviews*. London: Allen & Unwin, 1924, pp. 164–70.

———. *Remy de Gourmont, A Modern Man of Letters*. Seattle: University of Washington Chapbook, 1928.

Bencze, Eugène. *La Doctrine esthétique de Remy de Gourmont*. Toulouse: Aux Editions du Bon Plaisir, 1928.

Brunet, Gabriel. "Remy de Gourmont," *Ombres vivantes*. Paris: Editions "A l'Etoile," 1936, pp. 259–319.

Burke, Kenneth. "Adepts of 'Pure Literature,'" *Counter-Statement*. New York: Harcourt-Brace Co., 1931. Second edition, Los Altos, Calif.: Hermes Publications, 1953, pp. 21–37.

———. "De Gourmont on 'Dissociation,'" *A Rhetoric of Motives*. New York: Prentice-Hall, 1950, pp. 149–54.

Bussard, Lawrence H. "French Literary Criticism in the *Mercure de France*: 1890–1899." Unpub. doct. diss. University of Illinois, 1940.

Coffman, Stanley K., Jr. *Imagism: A Chapter for the History of Modern Poetry*. Norman: University of Oklahoma Press, 1951.

Coulon, Marcel. "La Complexité de Remy de Gourmont," *Témoignages*, 1re série. Paris: Mercure de France, 1910, pp. 141–209.

———. "Les Assises de Remy de Gourmont," *Témoignages*, 2me série. Paris: Mercure de France, 1911, pp. 75–169.

Eliot, T. S. (ed.). "Introduction," *The Literary Essays of Ezra Pound*. New York: New Directions, 1954.

———. "The Function of Criticism," "The Metaphysical Poets," and "Andrew Marvell," *Selected Essays, 1917–1932*. New York: Harcourt-Brace Co., 1932.

———. "Introduction," "The Perfect Critic," "Imperfect Critics," "Massinger," and "Tradition and the Individual Talent," *The Sacred Wood*. London: Methuen, 1928 ed.

Ellis, Havelock. "Remy de Gourmont." *From Rousseau to Proust*. Boston and New York: Houghton Mifflin, 1935, pp. 307–27.

Espey, J. J. "Physique de l'Amour," *Ezra Pound's Mauberley: A study in composition*. Berkeley: University of California Press, 1955, pp. 62–82.

France, Anatole. *La Vie littéraire*. Paris: Calmann-Levy, 1889–95, 4 vols.

Gosse, Edmund. "Two French Critics, Emile Faguet and Remy de Gourmont," *Aspects and Impressions*. New York: Scribners, 1922, pp. 203–23.

Gourmont, Jean de. *Souvenirs sur Remy*. Paris: Les Amis d'Edouard, no. 70, 1924.

Gourmont, Jean de, et Donne, Robert delle. *Bibliographie des oeuvres de Remy de Gourmont*. Paris: Les Bibliographies Nouvelles, 1922.

Greene, E. J. H. *T. S. Eliot et la France*. Paris: Boivin, 1951.

Hulme, T. E. *Notes on Language and Style*. Edited, with introduction, by Herbert Read. Seattle: University of Washington Chapbook, 1930.

———. *Speculations; essays on humanism and the philosophy of art*. Edited by Herbert Read. New York: Harcourt Brace, 1936.

Huneker, James. "Remy de Gourmont," *Unicorns*. New York: Scribners, 1917, pp. 18–32.

Jacob, P. E. "Remy de Gourmont," *University of Illinois Studies in Language and Literature*, vol. 16, No. 2, 1931, 176 pp.

Kenner, Hugh. *The Poetry of Ezra Pound*. New York: New Directions; London: Faber and Faber, 1951.

Léautaud, Paul. *Journal littéraire*, Vols. I and II. Paris: Mercure de France, 1954.

———. "Notes et souvenirs sur Remy de Gourmont," *Passe-Temps*. Paris: Mercure de France, 1929, pp. 101–20.

Lehmann, A. G. *The Symbolist Aesthetic in France, 1885–1895*. Oxford: Blackwell, 1950.

Lemaître, Jules. *Les Contemporains*. Paris: Société française d'imprimerie et de la librairie, 1898–1918, 4 vols.

Mossop, J. D. R. "Remy de Gourmont en Angleterre." Unpub. doc. diss. University of Paris (Sorbonne), 1949.

Murry, John Middleton. *The Problem of Style*. London: Oxford University Press, 1925.

O'Connor, William Van. *Sense and Sensibility in Modern Poetry*. Chicago: University of Chicago Press, 1948, Chapters V and VIII.

Peyre, Henri. "The Criticism of Contemporary Writing: A French View," in *Lectures in Criticism*, Bollingen Series XVI. New York: Pantheon Books, 1949, pp. 119–68.

———. *Writers and Their Critics: A Study of Misunderstanding*. Ithaca, N. Y.: Cornell University Press, 1944.

Pound, Ezra. "Remy de Gourmont, a Distinction Followed by Notes," *Instigations*. New York: Boni & Liveright, 1920, pp. 168–95. Reprinted in *Make it New*. New Haven: Yale University Press, 1935.

———. "Remy de Gourmont," Part I (reprinted from *Fortnightly Review*, 1915) and Part II (reprinted from *Poetry*, January 1916), *Pavannes and Divisions*. New York: Knopf, 1918, pp. 112–28.

———. *The Letters of Ezra Pound*. Edited by D. D. Paige. New York: Harcourt-Brace, 1950.

———. *The Literary Essays of Ezra Pound*. Edited with an Introduction by T. S. Eliot. New York: New Directions, 1954.

Rees, Garnet. *Remy de Gourmont, Essai de Biographie*

intellectuelle. Paris: Boivin, 1940. (Doctoral dissertation, Sorbonne, 1939.)

Regnier, Henri de. "Remy de Gourmont," *De mon Temps*. Paris: Mercure de France, 1933, 4th Ed., pp. 140–46.

Suckling, Norman. *Paul Valéry and the Civilized Mind*. London: Oxford University Press, 1955.

Taupin, René. *L'Influence du Symbolisme français sur la Poésie américaine (de 1910 à 1920)*. Paris: Champion, 1929.

Thibaudet, Albert. *Reflexions sur la critique*. Paris: Gallimard, 1939.

Voivenel, Paul. *Remy de Gourmont vu par son médècin. Essai de physiologie littéraire*. Paris: Editions du Siècle, 1924.

Articles

Aldington, Richard. "Modern Poetry and the Imagists." *Poetry*, June 5, 1914.

Bateson, F. W. "Contribution to a Dictionary of Critical Terms: 'Dissociation of Sensibility,'" *Essays in Criticism*, I, No. 3 (July 1951), 302–12.

Bateson, F. W., and Eric Thompson. [An exchange of letters on T. S. Eliot's "dissociation of sensibility."] *Essays in Criticism*, II, No. 2 (April 1952), 207–14.

Breunig, L. C. "F. S. Flint, Imagism's Maître d'Ecole," *Comparative Literature*, IV, No. 2 (Spring 1952), 118–36.

Brunetière, Ferdinand. "Le symbolisme contemporain," *Le Revue des Deux Mondes*, CIV, série 3 (March–April 1891), 681–92.

———. "Symbolisme et décadens [sic]," *La Revue des Deux Mondes*, XC, série 3 (November–December 1888), 213–26.

Burke, Kenneth. "Approaches to Remy de Gourmont," *Dial*, LXX (February 1921), 125–38. Reprinted in Burke's *Counterstatement* as part of "Three Adepts of Pure Literature." See above, Secondary Works, Books.

Denkinger, Marc. "Remy de Gourmont Critique,"
PMLA, LII, No. 4 (December 1937), 1147–60.

Imprimerie gourmontienne. A quarterly bulletin dedicated to Gourmont and edited by his friends. It appeared in ten numbers, from November 1, 1920, to the
beginning of 1925. It contains Gourmont's unpublished
fragments, reminiscences by his friends, a few studies,
and a bibliographical appendix.

Krutch, Joseph Wood. "The Nihilism of Remy de Gourmont," Nation, CXXVII (October 10, 1928), 357–58.

The Little Review, Remy de Gourmont Number, February–March 1919. This special issue contained the following articles: Richard Aldington, "De Gourmont, after
the Interim"; T. T. Clayton, "Le Latin mystique";
Frederic Manning, "M. de Gourmont and the Problem
of Beauty"; Ezra Pound, "De Gourmont: a Distinction"; and John Rodker, "De Gourmont—Yank."

Mossop, J. D. R. "Un Disciple de Gourmont: Richard
Aldington," Revue de Littérature Comparée, XXV
(1951), 403 ff.

Les Nouvelles Littéraires, May 10, 1924. A special number
dedicated to Remy de Gourmont, on the occasion of
the placing of a commemorative plaque on the building
where Gourmont had lived, 77 rue des Saints-Pères, in
Paris.

Taupin, René. "The Example of Remy de Gourmont,"
Criterion, X (July 1931), 614–25.

Turnell, Martin. "Literary Criticism in France [I and II],"
Scrutiny, VIII (September and December 1939), 167–
83, 281–98. Reprinted in R. W. Stallman (ed.),
Critiques and Essays in Criticism. New York: Ronald
Press, 1949, pp. 421–48.